A POCKETFUL
of ACORNS

Broadway Tower, Worcestershire

*All proceeds from the sale of this book will be
devoted to the work of the John Moore Society*

A POCKETFUL of ACORNS

A Selection of the
Country Articles of John Moore

Edited by Phillip Robbins
Illustrated by John Nursey

HiP
HISTORY INTO PRINT

First published by
History into Print, 56 Alcester Road,
Studley, Warwickshire B80 7LG in 2009
www.history-into-print.com

ISBN: 978-1-85858-334-1

The moral right of the author has been asserted

A Cataloguing in Publication Record
for this title is available from the British Library

Typeset in Sabon
Printed in Great Britain by
Cromwell Press Group

The cover photograph is of Bredon Hill
Photo courtesy of John Nursey

Contents

*To my wife Jane whose love and bravery
enabled this volume to be finished.*

Introduction

Mark Twain writes in his book *The Adventures of Tom Sawyer* "There comes a time in every rightly constructed boy's life when he has a raging desire to go somewhere and dig for buried treasure".

Having entered stoically into middle age without so much as sighting a promising 'Desert Island' I had all but given up hope until the halcyon day when our Chairman, John Shakles, led me to a cardboard box containing photocopies of most, if not all, of the articles written over many years by John Moore for various newspapers and magazines.

I must confess that I never thought that my treasure would be in a 'chest' previously owned by Messrs Sainsbury or that my 'Desert Island' would be man-made Redditch! I do not recall who went to the considerable trouble of reproducing all of these items, but I do know that they were forced to use a pioneer photocopier as some, black with carbon, were hard to decipher. Whoever it was deserves the highest praise as they have preserved them in an easily accessible form for posterity.

Copies of the articles sent to John Moore by his press agency, were cut out and meticulously pasted into his scrapbook but due to a serious flood at Lower Mill Farm (The Waters under the Earth) not all have survived.

John Moore wrote short items throughout his life. Some of these predate his first book, Dixon's Cubs, and I'm sure gave him a leg-up in his literary career. The last of these articles was published in the Birmingham Evening Mail a day after his death on July 27th 1967.

The Society, through its editor, has sought to use a selection of these in our bi-annual journal but even after 21 years it is clear that another generation would be required to publish them all.

I have always thought that the articles were worthy of being collected in book form. Very few of the articles have been edited, but merely reproduced as originally published – John Moore was very much his own editor, having to fit within the bounds of his employer's requirements.

One thing that may be said with certainty is that the quality of John Moore's work continues to shine throughout. It has been a pleasure producing this book. Fine writers, such as Moore, need to be remembered.

I am grateful to John Nursey for typing up the text and doing the pen and ink illustrations. These are largely of general country subjects and locations relevant to the area and are included purely to add general interest to the book. Some of the locations in the Tewkesbury area are as they would have looked in John Moore's time. I am consequently grateful to Maggie Thornton, Curator of the Tewkesbury Museum, who has made available photographs on which these particular sketches have been based.

It is the Society's hope that in time it will be possible to publish a further selection of the John Moore articles.

Phillip Robbins
Hon Secretary
John Moore Society

Whose was it?
His who is gone.
Who shall have it?
He who will come.
What shall we give for it?
All that we have.

Arthur Conan Doyle

Goose V for Victory

Walking home one night from our local, I heard the geese going over high up in the cold sky. I think it is one of the most exciting sounds I know.

It was one of those moonlit, frosty nights that Cecil Day Lewis describes most perfectly in a poem:

Hard are the nights now;
The fields at moonrise turn to agate,
Shadows are cold as jet;
In dyke and furrow, in copse and faggots
The frost's tooth is set,
And stars are the sparks whirled out by the north wind's fret.
On the flinty nights now.

Out of the cold emptiness up there among the stars came suddenly at first a sort of breathless clamour, as if there were a pack of hounds hunting hard on the brush of the north wind.

Honking

Then as the invisible gaggle came closer the hound-cry changed to that marvellous unmistakeable honking which seems to speak of Spitzbergen and the wastes of the Arctic.

It always gives me a prickle at the nape of the neck when I listen to it – the same sort of prickle one gets from hearing great poetry.

I couldn't see the geese. They were riding high on the wind's back, almost out of sight I daresay; but from the sound I could tell that there was a great flock of them – maybe a hundred or more, flying wingtip to wingtip in two or three big V-formations.

Once, at a dark moment in the last war, when I was flying a Walrus over the North Sea, my navigator spotted such a flock of wild geese coming towards us out of the dusk.

I was flying very low over the white seahorses, looking for mines ahead of a coastal convoy. The geese passed right over us, a thousand feet up; three formations, each making a perfect V for Victory.

My navigator grinned, and held up his thumb. And because the time was so dark and dangerous, I was only too willing to see omens in the sky. so I turned my thumbs up too; and heartened we flew on over the darkening green of the sea.

❈   ❈   ❈

Those were greylags, I think, the big lavender-grey ones which were probably the ancestors of our domestic geese.

The old, fat waddlers on the Common today could not lift themselves off the ground, let alone be borne upon the north wind over the sleeping countryside.

But when they are excited they make much the same sound as the wild greylags do, *ackh, ackh.*

Then suddenly the noise becomes loud again, rises to a sudden yelp, and once again in your imagination the geese are not geese but the hounds of heaven, a-hunting up among the stars.

The geese I heard the other night were probably white-fronts; these are the commonest wild geese in our part during the winter.

They have been called 'Laughing Geese' because every now and then, as they fly over, their harsh, loud, regular cry seems to die away and become, for a few seconds, a sort of low chuckle.

The early Wairm got the Bird

To revisit the scene of some childhood happiness is generally profitless and sometimes painful; you feel like a ghost. I knew this well. Nevertheless, as the fish weren't taking I thought I would risk it so I changed my spinner for an ordinary hook, which had lain at the bottom of my fishing bag for goodness knows how many years, and took the path to the Old Mill.

I thought I would collect a hank of that green silkweed which grows on waterfalls climb on to the sweeps of the old mill-wheel, and fish for chub in the swift water below the floodgates. If I had no luck I would cross the bridge to the weir, find a worm somehow, catch a minnow and use the minnow to catch a perch. This was the way I used to fish in my boyhood, and there were always a few perch to be had out of the back-eddies of the weir.

I was aware of my folly as soon as I got to the Old Mill. Some 30 years ago when I was 10, the miller had lived there with a great sandy cat. Both had watched my antics on the slippery waterwheel with kindly amusement and the cat had gobbled up my tribute of an occasional tiddler with just as much of a "Thank you" as an 18th century parson gave for his tithe.

But the white-hatted miller and his cat were gone the way of all flesh, the mill was derelict, and the River Board had erected new flood-gates there. I could see plenty of silkweed below the sill of these flood-gates and I was pretty sure there would be a chub in the tumbling waters.

It was impossible, however, to fish from the gates or the wall, because the whole establishment was surrounded by a stout iron fence, with the spikes bent outwards, and there was a bold notice on the fence which said, with that extraordinary rudeness which we learned from go-getting Americans, KEEP OUT.

As I walked over to the weir I reflected that the so-called Wicked Landlords of my childhood, with all their keepers and their "Trespassers will be Prosecuted" boards, were not half so possessive about their property as a modern corporation or nationalised undertaking. They were a bit touchy about their game, of course, but they never troubled their heads about small boys fishing for tiddlers.

Indeed in all my bug-hunting, birds-nesting, tiddler-catching boyhood I think I was never once refused permission to go where I wanted if I took the trouble to ask, and only two or three times was I chivvied away when I didn't ask. Certainly none of the old landlords would have put up a board saying simply KEEP OUT; they had better manners.

It made me angry, and perhaps there was some vestige of the vanished boy imprinted still on my mind. Anyhow, I decided not to keep out. I went to the nearest fisherman and begged from him a worm.

※   ※   ※

My hook of course, was much too big for minnow-catching; but this didn't matter. The child's trick is to dangle the worm in the water until the minnow has fastened its jaws upon it and then very slowly to pull it up. Sometimes he lets go; but often he doesn't. Any boy can thus fill a jam jar with minnows in half an hour. The Birmingham men watched the proceedings without comprehension.

"E's copped a minnie," they said, "with that wairm."

I put the minnow on my hook and proceeded to climb over the barbed wire. And now a rather disturbing thing happened. I found I was being shouted at, not by some official of the River Board, but by my fellow-fishermen themselves.

"Hey, you can't go in thay-er," they cried. "It says KEEP OUT."

That was the tragedy. They had accepted without question the validity of the notice. They had kept out; and they were utterly shocked by, and resentful of, the anarch who, at great risk to the seat of his pants was climbing in.

Into this orderliness have we fallen; possibly because we spend so much of our time standing in queues. When I caught my perch (first throw with the minnow, under the remembered campsheathing) I was identified in the fishermen's mind with a jumper of queues; and they howled at me.

※　　※　　※

I tore my trousers climbing back, but it was worth it; and I enjoyed, too, my interview with the inevitable functionary of the River Board who arrived, pushing a lawnmower, at the moment when I was disentangling myself from the wire. He was a very serious man whose only duty, as far I could make out, was the regulation of the flood-gates and the tending of the lawn.

He talked darkly of by-laws and prosecutions, but was otherwise extremely patient, explaining to me as if I were a child exactly why the barbed wire and the ill-mannered notice had been erected by his thoughtful employers.

"We put it up," he said severely, "to prevent people falling in."

We have become then, I thought a nation of nationalised nursemaids. I looked back across the years at the 10-year-old climbing on the waterwheel, the bamboo rod in one hand, the other clutching the slimy paddles; and smiled.

A Nostalgic Brew of Beer

I was reading John Nyren's *Cricketers of My Time* which was written I think about 1840 when I came upon his description of a match played on Broad Halfpenny between the famous Men of Hambledon and All England. "How these fine, brawn-faced fellows of farmers would drink to our success!" exclaimed Nyren, and went on to particularise what they would drink.

"Punch! Not your modern cat-lap milk punch – punch bedevilled – but good, unsophisticated John Bull stuff – stark! – that would stand on end – punch that would make a cat speak! Sixpence a bottle! The ale too! – not the modern horror under the same name, that drives as many men melancholy-mad as the hypocrites do – not the beastliness of these days, that will make a fellow's inside like a shaking hog – and as rotten; but barley-corn such as would put the souls of three butchers into one weaver. Ale that would flare like turpentine – genuine Boniface."

※   ※   ※

We can forgive him the superfluity of exclamation-marks if the beer was as good as all that. But let us turn now to the Welsh bard Sion Tudor, who was also extremely fond of beer and who wrote his poems, if I may make a guess, about 300 years before Nyren was born.

He held that the only beer which was worth drinking was the beer he had drunk in *his* own youth; but as for the stuff they give you nowadays, he said (nowadays being about 1560), why it's enough to make a poet sick.

Almost every time he called at a pub he was inspired by nausea to make up a poem about the bad beer, which he scrawled with a quartz upon the window pane as a warning to wayfarers who might follow him, thus:

Chester ale! Chester ale! I could ne'er get it down.

'Tis made of ground ivy, of dirt, and of bran:
'Tis as thick as a river below a huge town!
'Tis not lap for a dog, far less drink for a man!

Ground ivy, a little creeping green herb with purplish-blue flowers, was used for flavouring ale – for making it "bitter" – before the use of hops became common; or by brewers who thought the purchase of hops was an unnecessary extravagance.

❀ ❀ ❀

A Cotswold barn

George Borrow, walking through Wales in the footsteps of Sion Tudor, had the misfortune to call at an inn where the landlady was of such a cheeseparing nature, and where the beer brewed with ground-ivy was almost as sharp as wormwood.

" 'This is very bad ale,' I said.

" 'It ought to be very good,' said she, 'for I brewed it myself,' "So I told her; 'The goodness of ale does not so much depend upon who brews it as on what it is brewed of.' "

One up to George Borrow. But isn't it strange that these three hearty beer drinkers who flourished at different times, the great cricketer, the peripatetic bard, and the scholar gypsy who wrote *Lavengro,* should *each* have held the view that the beer of their youth was a nectar compared with the cat-lap of their later years?

"A modern horror," said John Nyren in the 1840's; "Thick as a river," said Sion Tudor some 50 years before Shakespeare created Falstaff; "Wormwood," snapped George Borrow, in 1860; and so on.

❋   ❋   ❋

And I'm prepared to bet that if I go down to the local tonight and get into conversation with the old men, it will not be very long before I hear three or four familiar phrases which fall from their lips as inevitably as the leaves fall from the trees every autumn.

"Evenin's be drawing in," they'll say.

"Ah."

"Christmas seems to come round quicker every year," they'll say.

"'Tis so as we git older."

"Christmas ain't what it wur."

"Nor's the beer neither. Swipes! Cat-lap! Ditch-water and kemmicals! Why, when I wur a lad... ."

A Language in which
Old and Young can meet

A townsman who apparently wakes up earlier than most tells me how fascinated he is by the market reports for farmers which are given on the wireless at about 6.45 in the morning.

The names of the different classes of creatures delight and bewilder him. A hogget sounds as if it were a little pig, but turns out to be a sheep; but tegs and theaves are also sheep, and pigs include gilts and cutters as well as baconers and porkers...

Splendid names

Then there are the rather splendid names of potatoes, 'Majestics and Arran Banners grown in silt'. My townsman lies in bed and muses romantically about the countryside, knowing nothing of the muck in the gateways and the frost on the sprouts which have to be picked for market.

※   ※   ※

But of course he is right; there is a whole farmyard vocabulary, mostly as old as the English language, which would be double-dutch to a town-dweller.

As a country child I learned it almost as soon as I could speak. The miskin, or mixen, was the dung-heap in which my small hands grubbed for the little red worms that are best for roach fishing; I was astonished to find how hot it was inside.

Recognised now

Straw was tied into 'boltings'; and a 'thrave' was four of them. Sockage (which I recognise now as 'soakage') was liquid manure.

A shuppick was a pitchfork – and you need a practised eye to see that the word is simply *sheaf-pike*.

A stank was a dam which we made so that we could store water in the brook during dry weather. Staddles were the stones which hayricks stood upon.

Squitch was couch-grass, and a squitch-fire therefore a bonfire of good-for-nothing rubbish.

When I was six or so I used all these words, and pronounced them 'correctly', i.e. 'not lahdidah'.

That is to say I would call a gatepost yatpwuist, or announce that there was a shyup dyud at the bottom of t'medder. I wish I'd kept my native speech; it is only when I'm talking to old countryman that I find myself slipping back into it today.

❖ ❖ ❖

Another collection of words and phrases which I learned then, and treasure still, consists of those which belong to the queer twilight of understanding in which the very old and the very young can meet and communicate with each other – the world of children and grannies, where both describe a tea-kettle as shooky, a cowslip ball as a tosty-ball, guilder roses as whissun-bosse, a piece of sore, ragged skin at the quick of a nail as 'a backfriend', and so on.

Children's names

To this world belongs the very apt children's name for the seed-capsules of the mallow, or the larger ones of the hollyhock. 'Cheese' we would call them, and indeed they were just the shape of a Double Gloster.

Chusha-wagga, by the way was our term for the pale cheese made from skim-milk; and for some reason which I shall never understand we spoke of the first, delightfully green, crisp little leaves on the hawthorn as 'bread and cheese'.

Bunting's song

The yellow bunting sang to us 'A little bit of bread and no cheese' – and does to me still.

Our oddest phrase of all described the effect when reflected sunlight or moonlight was thrown on the ceiling from the surface of, say, water in a bowl, or a looking glass.

We call it 'Jack-a-making-pancakes,' with the aptness and exquisite imagery which only a child or a poet can achieve, when either sees some phenomenon for the very first time.

Market Hall,
Chipping Campden

Fed by a Cat

One of our cats caught a pigeon and distributed its feathers over most of the house. This reminded me of the pleasant story concerning one Sir Henry Wyatt when he was confined in the Tower of London during the reign of Richard III.

Sir Henry, having foolishly involved himself in politics when politics were a pretty rough business, had been racked in the presence of the king himself and had mustard and vinegar poured down his throat.

He was then confined in a small noisome cell which had one tiny aperture through which he could see the sky.

His gaolers hadn't bothered to give him any food and he owed his survival, he said, to a kindly cat which caught him a pigeon every day and dropped it into his cell through the embrasure.

Superstition

History doesn't relate how long he survived upon his diet of pigeon. There is a local superstition in my part of the world that if you eat a pigeon a day for a week the cumulative effect of so much pigeon will kill you.

However, I know this is not true. A great character in the days of my youth, the old Colonel whom I have often written about, decided to see if there was anything in it.

He duly ate his pigeon a day for a week and then strode triumphantly into the local pub and lapsed into Gloucestershire as he always did on these occasions; 'Well, I beyunt jud, be I?'

He was experimental about everything; for example, if anybody told him a toadstool was poisonous he would eat it to find out, having first fortified himself against the poison with plenty of neat whisky which he believed to be an antidote against anything.

He drank about half a bottle once in anticipation of experimentally devouring a supper of those horrible orange-red toadstools (the colour of a recently fashionable lipstick).

"That'll quell 'em," he said. "That'll keep 'em quiet!" and sure enough, he was none the worse.

I have since learned that these toadstools are somewhat poisonous, so he was a lucky fellow!

A lover

So was Sir Henry Wyatt a lucky fellow to find a cat as faithful as Dick Whittington's. Luck seemed to run in his family; his son, Sir Thomas, was sent to the Tower twice by Henry VIII once for treason and the second time on suspicion of being one of the lovers of Anne Boleyn.

Heaven knows how Sir Thomas got away with that one, but he did, and he survived to write some excellent poetry.

His father, the story goes, was grateful to the cat tribe ever afterwards. His contemporaries observed in wonder; 'He would make as much of cats as other men would of spaniels'.

Semi-wild

Affection for cats was thought of as rather an oddity in Tudor times – dogs were more popular, and cats for the most part, were regarded as semi-wild beasts with which the dog owners liked to enjoy some barbarous sport.

Certainly Shakespeare did speak of 'the harmless, necessary cat' but there is no other evidence that he was fond of cats although he certainly was no lover of dogs either.

He simply detested spaniels, and three or four times he wrote in contempt of their fawning ways.

Their value

It is rather surprising to find the cat so neglected in Elizabethan literature when one thinks of the great esteem in which cats were held much earlier.

For example, in Wales during the Middle Ages, when the prince Hywel Dda made a whole series of laws designed for their protection, laying down their value and setting down various penalties for those who stole or killed them,

For example:-

The worth of the cat from the night it is kittened until it shall open its eyes is a legal penny. And from that time until it shall kill mice, two legal pence.

And after it shall kill mice, four legal pence and so it always remains.

The prince's own cats were naturally regarded as more valuable than anybody else's. Anyone who stole them, if he were caught, had to make recompense with 'a milch sheep with her lamb and her wool.'

There seems to have been a considerable trade in cats at that time because when you sold one it was assumed you guaranteed it, as it were, 'sound in wind and limb' and of good behaviour:

Whosoever shall sell a cat is to answer for her not going caterwauling every moon; and that she devour not her kittens; and that she hath ears, eyes, teeth and claws, and being a good mouser.

Enjoy each Season for Itself

As I walked back from the post the other evening, our lane was loud with bird-song. It was mild enough to set the gnats dancing in the lee of the hedges; and song thrush and blackbird, robin and jenny-wren were kidded by the soft air into thinking it was spring.

What a contrast with this time last year, when the snow lay deep along the lane side, and the frost bit deep and hard, and instead of that jargoning in the treetops, all was silent as the grave!

Changed meaning

Jargoning? By all means: it comes from the French verb *Jargonner*, meaning to warble (used of birds, not of humans).

Chaucer uses it in this sense in 'The Canterbury Tales'; and so does Coleridge in a beautiful, eerie verse in 'The Ancient Mariner'...

> *I heard the skylark sing.*
> *Sometimes all little birds that are,*
> *How they seem'd to fill the sea and air*
> *Sometimes a-dropping from the sky*
> *With their sweet jargoning!*

Gradually, during the last century, the word has changed its meaning to 'unintelligible speech,' and nowadays we mainly use it in such phrases as 'legal jargon' to describe the rigmaroles of lawyers, which are much less agreeable than was the concert of blackbird and thrush in our lane by the churchyard on that unseasonably soft evening.

'We'll pay'

And of course, I met an old so-an-so, who reminded me; "Us'll pay for it later on!"

I have observed before this dismal Puritanism of the English countryman, who cannot enjoy a sweet day out of season without reminding himself, and everybody else he meets, that we shall probably have to suffer frosts in May.

So we shall, possibly; but to other than the Praisegod Barebone sort, that makes it none the less pleasant to feel a soft Atlantic wind on a February day, and a blink of sun which raises the mercury to 50 degrees, so that the first bees start humming.

And the first crocus, like a candle-flame against the brown earth!

It makes me want to throw my hat in the air.

But not so Praisegod Barebone. "We'll pay for it later on, thee see if us don't!"

All seasons

But then I like all weathers, seasonable or no. A blustering March wind, a frosty dawn with the cobwebs all tinsel, showers in proud-pied April, with the clouds high-flying, soft summer rain that makes you smell the flowers and the earth...

Let me quote Coleridge again:

Therefore all seasons shall be sweet to thee
Whether the summer clothe the general earth
With greenness, or the redbreast sit and sing
Betwixt the tufts of snow on the bare branch
Of mossy apple-tree, while the nigh thatch
Smokes in the sun-thaw; or whether eave-drops fall
Heard only in the trances of the blast,
Or if the secret ministry of frost
Shall hang them up in silent icicles,
Quietly shining to the quiet moon.

Marvellous, marvellous lines. 'The secret ministry of frost' – what a phrase!

And that 'Quietly shining to the quiet moon.' How keenly and eagerly Coleridge felt the seasons; and how happy (by comparison with Barebones) is the man who can enjoy them all – 'A man for all seasons', like Sir Thomas More!

Tapsalteerie English?

I have been re-reading my Robert Burns and trying hard to conquer the prejudice which the very sight of printed Scottish dialect excites in the Southerner. There is a real difficulty of language. Take this verse, for instance, from *The Twa Herds*:

> *The thummart, willcat, brock, an'tod*
> *Weel kend his voice thro' a' the wood.*
> *He smelled their ilka hole an' road,*
> *Baith out an' in;*
> *An' well he lik'd to shed their bluid*
> *An' sell their skin.*

It is, in fact, excellent poetry; but first of all you have to know that 'thummart' means polecat, 'willcat' is wild cat of course, 'brock' is badger, 'tod' is fox. Next you have to realise that there is woolliness, an imprecision about Scottish vowel-sounds, which makes the rhymes of 'tod', 'wood', 'road' and 'bluid' perfectly acceptable.

I know that a courageous Englishman, Mr. Kean Seymour, has recently translated Burns's poetry into English; but a verse such as the one I have quoted would surely lose all its magic in the process. The native Scottish words are woven into the poetry; and what glorious words some of them are! 'Sonsie', for example, in that piece of doggerel *To a Haggis*.

> *Fair fa' your honest sonsie face*
> *Great chieftain o' the puddin race!*

Apparently it contains the meanings of jolly-comely-plump all rolled into one; we have nothing that quite matches it in English. I like 'sonsie'. And I like 'tapsalteerie' for topsy-turvy, and 'hogshouther' for horse play and 'whigmaleeries' for the crotchets, and 'skelpielimmer' which defeats all dictionaries and is described as 'a technical term in female scolding'.

Of course all dialect written down has a frightening and putting-off appearance. The Dorset poetry of William Barnes is for me utterly unreadable and indeed repulsive to the eye; for example:–

> *Since you noo mwore be at my zide,*
> *In walks in summet het,*
> *I'll goo alwone where mist do ride,*
> *Droo trees a-drippen wet...*
> *Since I do miss your vaice and feace*
> *In prayer at eventide.*
> *I'll pray wi' woone sad vaice for greace*
> *To goo where you do bide...*

It may be poetry; *The Oxford Book of English Verse* thinks so; but although I live much closer to Dorset that to Ayr I can get more sense and more pleasure out of Burns. Indeed I have an unworthy suspicion that this is not so much the true speech of Dorset countrymen as what a mild and kindly parson-cum-poet thought it ought to be.

It has no essential guts; there's no strength to it; and the speech of countrymen, whether they live in Ayrshire or Gloucestershire or Sussex, seems to me to possess always a sort of gnarled and knotty quality, a roughness, a toughness, a vigour. Barnes's version of Dorset is somehow emasculated. Compare it with these few sentences, from Cheshire, which I quote from *A County Parish* by A. W. Boyd:

> *The weather wor gleamy, rabl and puthery, and after mizzlin'*
> *a bit it had turned into a reet drabbly day and Bob wor weary, for*
> *th' mare had turned gafty and had wauted th'cart o'er and broken*
> *the ridg'uth. He'd been burnin' rucks of teetur-wyzles and brash*
> *cut with a slanching-hook from the quicks; he'd carted chats and*
> *ackersprit teeturs to th' pigs and fashes to th' bastes; he'd been*
> *chuckin' fother dain from th' bauks to th' bing with a pikel and*
> *cleanin' out the booses in th' shippon till he got clawped wi'*
> *muck. The fowl wor aw' flaskert and prating because a rot had*
> *scrawled into the hen-hurdle and he'd set a trap for that....*

Now although I'm Gloucestershire, and that comes from Great Budsworth in the neighbourhood of Northwich, I can understand it easily. Some of the words are unfamiliar, but it has a recognisable rhythm; it growls, it grumbles with the authentic rise and fall of a countryman's voice.

And what fun it is! What splendid strong nouns it has, like 'teetur-wyzles', what expressive adjectives like 'ackersprit', what powerful verbs like 'clawped'. Compare it with William Barnes' vacuous yammering and note the difference. But compare it with Burns, and you will recognise at once a kind of likeness, because in both cases real countrymen are speaking in the tongue of their fathers, vigorous, vivid, of the earth earthy, the speech of peasants and poets, and ploughmen who are both.

❀　❀　❀

GLOSSARY – Gleamy, hot and showery; **puthery,** hot and close; **mizzlin',** fine rain; **drabbly,** steady rain; **gafty,** jibbing; **wauted,** overturned; **ridg'uth,** chain which supports the shafts; **brash,** hedge-loppings; **slanching,** trimming; **quicks,** hawthorns; **rucks,** heaps; **teetur-wyzles,** potato-tops; **fashes,** turnip-tops; **chats,** small potatoes; **ackersprit,** potatoes with small extra tubers; **bastes,** cattle; **fother,** fodder; **bauks,** hay-loft; **bing,** passage in front of cows' stalls; **shippon,** cowshed; **clawped** daubed; **aw'** all; **pikel,** hay-fork; **booses,** cowstalls; **flaskert,** bewildered and fluttery; **rot,** rat; **scrawled,** crawled; **hen-hurdle,** hen-roost over a pig-sty.

Spirit of England

I was reminded yesterday of Tennyson's lines in his poem called 'The Gardener's Daughter'

> *Those eyes*
> *Darker than darkest pansies, and that hair*
> *More black than ash buds in the front of March.*

How keenly Tennyson marked the signs of the seasons! He knew how uncompromising and wintry the ash buds look at this time of the year; sullen, tight-fisted as Scrooge, refusing to admit the promise round the corner whatever the first honey bees humming round the gold of the pussy willow may say.

Not a prophesy

It may well be a couple of months yet before the ash puts on its leaves, but when it does, the old fellows won't fail to notice, saying *"Ash before oak, us'll get a soak,"* or *"Oak Before ash, us'll have a splash"* as the case may be.

Some experts say that the rhyme should be read not as a prophecy but as an observation. If we have had a wet spring, the deep-rooted oak will leaf first; if we've only had a splash the shallow-rooted ash will have the advantage.

But what a lovely tree it is when the green fronds, at long last, spring forth from it.

I love the ash-tree – as Cobbett did. He sang its praises, in 'Rural Rides,' for hardihood against the winds, for the tall beauty of its stem and for the loveliness of its leaves, for underwood and timber and for firewood.

> *As new or ash old*
> *Is fit for a queen with a crown of gold*

runs an old rhyme.

It is surely the only wood that will give you an intensely hot fire even if you burn it within days of its being cut. I have seen foresters cooking their breakfast on the trimmings of a newly-felled ash-tree.

Ash timber used to be valuable when the world ran on wooden wheels. Coaches and carts and farm wagons depended on it.

The first motor-car bodies were built of it; and during the first world war those daring, dicey aeroplanes were made of it, and the agents of the Government sought high and low for ash along the hedgerows and by the woodsides, all over England.

Best handles

The little coppice shoots in ash-plantations have always provided the best walking-sticks, broomsticks, hop-poles, spars, tool handles, hoops and (I believe) hockey-sticks, too; for the wood is tough and elastic. It 'gives' but does not break.

Now that I come to think of it, I cannot remember having seen an ash felled by the wind, although the tree is so shallow-rooted. Indeed you hardly ever come across a fallen ash-tree unless the saw has been at it.

If they are spared, the ancient ones will shed a few branches every season and die by inches over the long years

> Old soldiers never die,
> They only fade away.

The ash, in fact, is one of those trees which, in a mysterious way, seem to express the very spirit of the English countryside.

Let me end with a Kipling quotation, as I began with one from Tennyson. It comes from his 'Tree-Song'.

> Of all the trees that grow so fair
> Old England to adorn,
> Greater are none beneath the sun
> Than Oak and Ash and Thorn...
> England shall bide till Judgement Tide
> By Oak and Ash and Thorn.

Mother kept the Goblins away

For me, because I am an incurable optimist, the spring generally begins some time between Candlemas and St. Valentine's Day.

Generally; that is to say that in about three seasons out of five I shall find a snowdrop and a yellow crocus and see the lamb-tails on the hazels turning from greenery-yallery to bright ochre and see the twigs on the sallows glowing in the wan sun, a colour I can't describe, somewhere between pale amber and orangey-red.

And with reasonable luck I shall see the first humble bee and I shall know the temperature at midday has reached 50 degrees because no bee in his senses would ever come out unless the temperature is 50 degrees.

Old-fashioned

In my part of the Midlands we speak of snowdrops as Candlemas Bells because they are almost always in flower at this season.

We always have an argument concerning Candlemas Day – whether or not it is the day when you should take down your Christmas decorations.

Modern housewives, hating the dustiness of decorations hung too long, usually have them down on Twelfth Night, but my mother who was old-fashioned, greatly disapproved of this and would never dream of burning the holly and the mistletoe until the 2nd of February.

Old authority seems to be on my mother's side. Here's Robert Herrick, the parson-poet, writing in the 1650's:

> *Down with the Rosemary and so*
> *Down with the Holly, Ivy, all*
> *Wherewith ye dress the Christmas Hall:*
> *That so the superstitious find*
> *No one least branch there left behind;*

For look how many leaves there be
Neglected there (maids, trust to me),
So many Goblins you shall see.

We were never troubled by goblins in my mother's house during the days of my youth – she saw to that.

The mistletoe bough, every sprig of holly, the decked Christmas tree itself, must remain until Candlemas Day exactly where she had set them on Christmas Eve; and then – not a day later – they must be put on the bonfire.

Courtship

As for St. Valentine's of course, its special association with the spring is the old idea that the birds started their courtship on February 14.

Hail, Bishop Valentine, whose day this is
All the air is thy diocese

wrote John Donne in a delightful poem in which he described the robin as 'the household bird with the red stomacher.'

Unfortunately the naturalists give no support to the idea that the birds mate on St. Valentine's; most of them are troubled by no such thoughts until at least a month later.

Nature god

But human beings did once upon a time choose mates for themselves, however, temporary, round about February 14.

The feast was then called the Lupercalia; it was held in Rome and indeed over all Southern Europe in honour of a god called Lupercus, which was simply another name for Faunus, a nature god of the Romans.

The particular feature which made the Lupercalia so agreeable to the young men and women of Rome was a sort of love lottery as you might call it, a super Paul Jones.

The priests of Lupercus put the names of the young women into one box and the names of the young men into another box and drew them out in pairs.

Paired up thus by chance, the young people were free to enjoy themselves during the Lupercalia as best they could.

Of course, one could imagine chance working unfavourably; but young men and young women do sometimes cheat in a Paul Jones and I dare say a small tip to the priest would ensure that your particular Poppela, or whoever it might be, would be yours.

'Lewd custom'

Much of our country folklore concerning St. Valentine's seems to spring from the Lupercalia in ancient Rome.

Although the Church set out 'to abolish the heathen, lewd superstitious custom of boys drawing the names of girls' and to 'change it into giving billets with the names of certain saints for them to honour and imitate', it is only too true, alas, that girls are preferred to saints by almost every young chap, and so as late as 1676 we find in Poor Robin's Almanack a pleasant little rhyme;

Now Andrew, Anthony and William,
For Valentines draw Prue, Kate, Jilian.

Stone stile on Bredon Hill

No Room for Grass and Daisies...

When you destroy a blade of grass,
You poison England at her roots.

So wrote the poet Gordon Bottomley; and now I read that the
Borough Council of Cheltenham, which still calls itself a Garden
Town, has decided to replace some of its grass verges with asphalt.

Instead of the green and living herb, which smells so fresh in
the spring, assuages the tired eye in summer, gives cheer even in
winter with its hint that something still grows – instead of that
ASPHALT! – the stuff which derives I suppose from that pitch-
lake in Trinidad which I once visited.

It presented a loathsome landscape, as if the atrabilious entrails
of the earth were indecently exposed to view, a black slime, itself the
negation of life, in which nothing could live or grow.

Looking at it, I thought of asphalt paths in mean North-country
towns, asphalt squares between prison walls where convicts
exercise, asphalt playgrounds of East End schools, asphalt 'areas'
haunted by the damp souls of Mr. T. S. Eliot's housemaids... But Ye
Gods! I never thought that Cheltenham would use it to smother the
little green spears that shoot in March.

Bureaucrats hate grass. They hate it because it grows, which is
itself an offence; for then it has to be cut, trimmed tidied – and as
we know the only passion which stirs the bureaucratic soul is a
passion for tidiness.

Not only does the grass grow, but certain intrusive herbs
which councils call weeds, but which you and I call flowers,
spring up among the grasses.

❁ ❁ ❁

Some of these plants are taller than others and this is another
cause of 'untidiness'. So great pains are taken to destroy them by
means of hormone weed-killers and the wayfarer is treated to a

spectacle of withered, shrivelled and dying vegetation which oddly enough is deemed preferable to the lacy umbels of the hedge-parsley, the gold cups of the buttercups, or the exquisite blue of the cranesbill.

Even daisies seem to be unpleasing to the bureaucratic eye. If you were in the Army during the war you surely remember the trouble which the bureaucrats in uniform took to get rid of the daisies from the sacred patch of lawn in front of the Officer's Mess.

❋   ❋   ❋

My own service, the Navy which you'd think might welcome the sight of a flower or two after looking at so much empty sea, was equally possessed by this extraordinary aversion to daisies. In late May 1940 I arrived at a training station ashore which hadn't really woken up to the fact that there was a war on, and I found a couple of defaulters, who might have been usefully employed to dig slit-trenches, crawling on their hands and knees outside the Ward Room digging up daisy-roots with pocket-knives.

As I stood watching them a white trail streaked across the sky. Then the sirens went, and the daisy-diggers nearly jumped out of their skins and scurried to the nearest air-raid shelter.

I wasn't ashore much after that until May 1944 when we were preparing to invade Normandy. There was a big lawn outside our invasion headquarters near Portsmouth; and blow me, when I looked out of my office window one morning, there were half a dozen defaulters, on their hands and knees, grubbing up daisies...

❋   ❋   ❋

Cheltenham, however, has gone one better than the tidy-minded soldiers and sailors. There won't be any daisies because there won't be any grass for them to grow in; and in this respect Cheltenham makes itself one with the barrack-square, with the prison-yard, and with that dreary town of Slough to which Mr. John Betjeman cheerfully invited Hitler's bombers at the beginning of the war:

Come, friendly bombs, and fall on Slough!
It isn't fit for humans now.
There isn't grass to graze a cow,
Swarm over, Death.

Old cottages at Bibury,
Gloucestershire

Parson's Folly, Bredon Hill

A Dull World without such Follies

One of the books I should like to write, but shall never have the time for, is a history of Follies – I do not mean the passing pranks that die with a man's memory but the solid, permanent, architectural Follies. which stand upon a hill and declare to the generations of wayfarers: The chap who built me was by ordinary everyday standards, more than a little mad.

There is great scope for such a book. I should like Dame Rose Macaulay, Dame Edith Sitwell or Mr. John Betjeman to write it. They all have the right mixture of sound scholarship and humorous understanding.

Inscriptions

It should tell us as much as is known about the Mad Lords, Megalomaniac Industrialists, and Eccentric Country Squires whose strange ambition for this particular kind of immortality led them to spend fortunes on their Follies.

It should record faithfully the inscriptions, written in bad Latin, which are generally to be found in Follies – inscriptions which being literally translated run as a rule rather like this:

> *JOHN BLANK, Armiger, anno. dom. MDCCLXVI, in the Reign of George The Third, did erect this tower, from which in favourable weather thou canst look, O Traveller, upon no less than six counties. This he did not for his own delight only, but for that of his neighbours, and of all people.*

☒ ☒ ☒

Some such towers are provided with telescopes chained to an upper window, or with instruments rather like sundials; marked not with the hour but with the names of such landmarks as are visible on a fine day; you can manipulate a handle which turns a pointer say to Worcester Cathedral or the Black Mountains.

Objectionable

I suppose if you had a very big estate it gave you a very lordly sense of ownership to climb up into the top of your own Folly and look all round, north, south, east and west, and say to yourself that as far as you could see it was all yours – except, perhaps, for that objectionable building away on the left built in such excruciating taste by your upstart neighbour!

I suppose, too, that in the days before aeroplanes there was a real pleasure (which we can no longer understand) in looking on the Coloured Counties from above.

We are pretty used to two-dimensional landscapes nowadays; and we find them dull. But for a man who had never flown it must have been an experience unusual and therefore interesting to perch upon the top of a very high, steep hill.

Most of our Follies were built in the 18th century; a few in the 19th, when their architectural style became very extraordinary indeed.

Obelisks were the fashion for a long time; but I can never encounter the word obelisk without dismay, because when I was a boy at prep. school we were sometimes sent on runs, which I dreaded, and the objective of the runs was almost always the Obelisk at Eastnor, on the southern slope of the Malvern Hills. '... *Such a gift from the gods as would amply justify the building of a magnificent Folly...*'

Muddy, breathless and miserable, at least twice every winter term I trotted resentfully towards this Obelisk and cursed the man who had put it up and so given to my schoolmasters the idea of making us run there.

❖   ❖   ❖

Bredon Hill has a pleasant Folly, a 'summer house' built at its highest point. It was put up I believe, because the landlord had realised that the top of the hill was only just short of 1,000 feet above sea level; his tower was designed of the appropriate height to remedy this omission on the part of nature.

Sociological prigs, of course, disapprove of Follies, seeing them as monuments to the wastefulness, vulgarity, and vainglory of the Idle Rich; but their oddity nevertheless enchants me and I think it would be a dull world that didn't contain such occasional foolishness.

Indeed it is already a dull world in that respect, for nobody builds Follies nowadays, not even the winners of £75,000 in football pools – such a gift of the gods as would, I should have thought, amply justify the building of a magnificent Folly upon the nearest available hill

Don't cut the Heads off our Poplars

I feel like starting a society for the Protection of Poplars. A splendid row of tall ones not far from where I live have had about 20 feet of their tops cut out. I can't conceive why, for these trees which stood in a hedgerow weren't shading anybody's garden or causing any inconvenience at all. It must have been quite an expensive operation, and not without danger, to saw out the tops of more than a dozen tall trees. I suspect that some men calling themselves 'tree doctors' may have called on the farmer and persuaded him that the poplars 'needed doing.'

One of the arguments which these glib fellows use is that 'Poplars always split unless they have the tops taken out of them.' They tried this on an innocent friend of mine who wasn't a countryman-born. At enormous cost he let them 'doctor' his well-grown poplar trees. They now look awful and will still look awful in ten years time! And, of course, poplars *don't* split if left to grow as the Almighty meant them to. You have only to look at the beautiful unlopped trees that grow alongside all the roads of France.

Some minor poet, whose name I've forgotten, wrote some verses which began: *God wrote his loveliest poem on that day He made the first tall poplar tree.* Such a tree should go up like a church spire, or like smoke on a dead still day. A truncated poplar is as sad to see as a de-horned Ayrshire cow.

Of course we know the reason for taking off those lovely sickle-shaped horns: the cattle can do a lot of damage to each other in gateways or at markets. But for the life of me I can't see the point of cutting off a poplar tree in its prime. It's the act of a barbarian,

❈   ❈   ❈

As readers of this column will guess my attitude to Puritans is somewhat like that of Sir Andrew Aguecheek:

MARIA: *Marry, sir, sometimes he is a kind of puritan.*
SIR ANDREW: *O, if I thought that, I'd beat him like a dog.*
SIR TOBY: *What, for being a puritan? Thy exquisite reason, dear knight?*
SIR ANDREW: *I have no exquisite reason for't, but I have reason good enough.*

Well, I've had reason good enough, during a season which gave us sweet violets and crocuses in January, blue days borrowed from April in early February, daffodil buds before Valentine's and such joyous birdsong as I've never heard before on winter mornings.

Everywhere I went I would meet, not once but half a dozen times a day, the typical English puritan bellyaching as usual: *Nice day, yes; but we shall pay for it later, you see if we don't.* I could beat him like a dog. Can you imagine a Frenchman or an Italian being such an old misery? He would surely accept with both hands, the wonderful, unexpected bounty of soft winds and early flowers which the good God poured forth for him.

Not so the Cromwellian English, nor the Calvanist Swiss, nor the John Knoxish Scots, nor the Lutheran Germans! Such cannot enjoy anything agreeable without reminding themselves and everybody whom they happen to meet that pains and punishments follow pleasure as surely as night follows day.

※　　※　　※

Not so very long ago there was a little sect of extreme puritans who lived in a village near mine. Among a hundred things they disapproved of was fishing on Sunday.

It happened that a narrow lane which led to the river ran past their tin-roofed chapel. When they came out of chapel on a Sunday morning they would love to walk very slowly, four or five of them abreast along this lane, holding up the cars and motorbikes of frantic fishermen, mad to get to the river, who hooted in vain behind them.

Father Time with his scythe has reaped those bearded misanthropes who, come to think of it, looked a bit like Father

Time themselves. I well remember their sour looks and melancholy voices, for when I was a boy they sternly rebuked me for butterfly catching on a Sunday.

I suppose their kind is dying out in England; but when I was abroad last year I met a Dutchman who told me of an old farmer in his village whose Sabbatanarianism was so implacable that well before midnight on Saturday he would take pains to shut up his cockerel away from the hens. Nor was it allowed back in their company until Monday dawned.

Bridge over the Windrush,
Bourton on the Water

Every Field has its Name

I met a townsman in a train who was genuinely astonished to learn that individual fields had names. He'd been staring out of the carriage window for half an hour or more, vaguely aware of fields of all shapes and sizes, square, oblong, oval, pentagonal, some pastured by cows, some planted with winter corn, some ploughed and lying fallow until the spring.

He could hardly believe it when I told him that every one of those enclosures bore a name known not only to its owner but to the men who worked in it and such other countrymen as had reason to walk over it; that in most cases the name was to be found on the deeds of the farm or estate; and that some of the names were hundreds of years old.

'What sort of names?' he asked me.

I told him a few; Cuckoo Pen, Fiddler's Folly, Cold Elm. The Forty Acre, Puppy's Playground, Breaking Stone Meadow, Whistling Down Hay, Mog Ditch, Parson's Piece, Long Furlong...

How they sing to us, these ancient and beautiful names by which our grandfathers and our great-grandfathers recognised footpath and landmark! The poet Edward Thomas (who was killed in the first war) put some of them in a verse;

> *If ever I should by chance grow rich*
> *I'd buy Codham, Cockridden and Childerditch,*
> *Roses, Pyrgo and Lapwater,*
> *And let them all to my elder daughter.*

And again;

> *If I were to own this countryside*
> *As far as a man in a day could ride.*
> *And the Tyes were mine for giving or letting –*
> *Wingle Tye, and Margaretting*
> *Tye – and Skreens, Gooshays, and Cockerells,*
> *Shellow, Rochetts, Bandish and Pickerells,*
> *Martins, Lambkins and Lillyputs.*

❊   ❊   ❊

Indeed if I were a farmer how proud I should be to own such a domain! Most farmers do. On the big Ordnance map hanging on the wall of the back room they quaintly call their 'office' the boundaries of each field are shown, the name inked in, and sometimes the area; 'Tom Taplow's Hollow, 6a 3r 4p.' Who was Tom Taplow? Nobody knows, though you might find out if you chiselled away the moss from one of the tombstones in the churchyard.

Sometimes a field is named after a past owner; sometimes because of a physical feature – for example, Little Twittocks, which I hazard meant a little field with three oaks in it; or because of some characteristic of the soil, for instance, Starveall, Hungry Hill, or Stony Bank.

Some of the names are poetic, some are obscure, some are funny, a few are Rabelaisian, Quite a few are grim – Dead Man's Acre, Gibbet Hill, Hangman's Hill, the Murder Piece, and so on.

In my own part of the world we have several Drinkers' Ends and Druggers' Ends. 'Ends,' of course, means usually the end of a lane or a road, as 'Dead End,' but who these Drinkers and Druggers were I have never been able to discover.

❊   ❊   ❊

The folk-lorists, a serious lot, generally seek to read more into a name than is really there. 'Foxwood,' for example, is quite straightforward. It is so named because it harboured foxes. But I met a learned folk-lorist who shook his head and said, "Ah. Foxwood. Very significant. That's a corruption of Folkswood, you know."

The 'folk,' of course, were the fairies. Some clever people derive 'foxglove' from "folk's glove" in the same way; but I doubt if the ordinary English countryman has ever concerned himself much with fairies, which are a conception somewhat alien to our way of thought.

That is not to deny that we are superstitious; ghosts and witches come into our place-names, and in some parts are believed in still.

But with all respect to Rudyard Kipling, whose *Puck of Pook's Hill* is one of the most delightful books ever written, I think the English countryman has generally shied away from the idea of fairies, believing them to be 'silly.'

❋　❋　❋

Pook's Hill, incidentally is a real place-name in Sussex. To make Puck its *genius loci* was possibly a brilliant piece of Kipling improvisation; at a guess I'd say it was more likely to have belonged once upon a time to a farmer called Pook. In any case the idea of Puck as a fantastic, mischievous and tricksy sprite is comparatively recent.

It probably dates from the *Midsummer Night's Dream*. The Puck in whom Old England half-believed was an *evil* spirit, a demon; but that, as Mr. Kipling himself would have said, is quite another story...

Chatter in the Sky

Nothing lifts my heart more, on a cold dark winter day, than the sight of a big flock of wild geese winging overhead. Their strange and somehow rather terrible cry speaks of the Arctic wastes and the great winds and the freedom of the skies. Indeed, the world is their oyster! – for in their spacious migrations they sweep to and fro across it.

A white-fronted goose ringed by Peter Scott in the Severn Estuary last February was reported from the Russian island of Kolguev on the 25th of May; another from Kursk in Southern Russia on the 4th of April. The Russians, incidentally, are meticulous in their reports of ringed birds, and I am told by an ornithologist that they are always most co-operative in sending us their scientific publications.

This is a fairly trivial matter, but perhaps it is possible to see a glimmer of hope in it. If at any rate some scientists on opposite sides of the Iron Curtain can get on together, it is a step in the right direction; and so far, thank goodness, nobody has discovered any ideological aspect to the study of birds.

❋　　❋　　❋

As soon as I hear the far faint chatter in the sky, and see the skeins flying southward, I am out on my river-meadows with my gun under my arm and the long cartridges loaded with big shot in its breech. It is scarcely a blood-sport because I hardly ever get a shot at the geese and if I kill one in a season I count myself lucky; it's the stalk that matters, and the pitting of my wits against their wildness. There is no bird more difficult to get near even if you wear white overalls on snowy days, as I do, and crawl up the ditches till you are soaked through with ice-cold slush.

I daresay I have voluntarily suffered more hardship in the pursuit of these birds than I had to put up with in the whole of the war. I ask myself why I do it, why I stand up to my waist in freezing water waiting for them at dusk, or get up at six on a January day to dig my little fox-hole on the east-coast saltings. (I once invited a friend to come with me on this annual holiday for the purpose of shooting white-fronted geese.) 'Not a white-fronted Houri of Paradise', he replied on a postcard, 'would get me out of bed at that time in the morning!'

❋   ❋   ❋

I suppose it fascinates me simply because it is uncomfortable and difficult; and on those very rare occasions when the hunter wins there is a real sense of triumph, it is a matter to celebrate with a bottle of burgundy. And, of course, because one shoots so few geese one can remember every triumph as if it happened yesterday – my first, white-front, for instance, which I shot on the ground at the age of 15, having nicked the cartridge case with my pocket-knife so that the shot came out solid like a bullet from an elephant-gun. (But do not try that trick, for it is extremely foolhardy, and I was lucky that the gun-barrel didn't blow up in my face.)

My second was a solitary greylag which flew straight over my head in broad daylight as if it offered itself as a sacrifice in order to teach a boy of 16 that birds should be shot on the wing. It came down in the river and I had to swim for it; but although there was cat-ice at the edge of the rushes I had a boy's exultation to warm me and I did not notice the cold.

My third goose nearly killed me. I had just learned to fly a Moth, and it occurred to me that I could give my friends a good chance of a shot if I did some low-flying over the meadows and chivvied the geese towards them. I dived on the flock from 2,000 feet, and the whole 200 suddenly rose up in a cloud towards me; at 50 feet. I was in the middle of them and there seemed to be wings and necks all round me.

Then there was a frightful bang, as if some important part of the aeroplane had snapped, and when I landed I found a dent two inches deep in the leading edge of the starboard wing. My friends (who didn't get a shot) picked up the goose later and told me it was nearly decapitated. If my propeller had hit it I should have had to make my first forced landing in a meadow intersected with deep dykes, and I don't think it would have been very successful!

❈   ❈   ❈

Once in a lifetime a fortunate man gets a right and left at wild geese. Mine came out of a blizzard on the coast of Wales, in the dusk when it was nearly too late to see them. Indeed I heard them for a full minute before I spotted them and by then I was nearly blinded by staring into the snowy whiteness.

There were a dozen or so in the flock and they were riding on the wind, necks thrown out talking very softly and eerily of Siberia and Spitzbergen. The powdery snow hurt my eyeballs as I shot, and then there were two falling together, spinning as they fell, like inside-out umbrellas, and they both came down at my feet.

That night we drank two bottles of Burgundy! But how many scores of times, I wonder, have I got cold and drenched for nothing, perhaps not even catching sight of a goose, or perhaps after a two-hours' stalk seeing them rise out of range and circle high overhead, soon to depart with what sounded like a faint chuckle, so remote that is seemed to come from the region of the cold stars!

The Trouble with Talpa Europaea

Six months ago, in this column, I was writing about 'population explosions.'

The sudden, inexplicable increase in numbers of some species of animal is followed invariably by an epidemic that decimates the species and often makes it temporarily quite rare.

At the moment we are much troubled by a population explosion among the moles.

Among market gardens they are doing serious damage. Old countrymen with long memories say there have never been so many moles within man's recollection.

Why? I have not heard a plausible explanation.

Unlike the rabbit the mole is not a very fast breeder. It is said to rear only one litter a year, there being four of five in a litter (but because it cannot easily be kept in captivity nobody knows much about the life history of the mole).

Few enemies

Its natural enemies are few, and it is well defended against them because of its burrowing habits and because its flesh is unpalatable to many predators.

A few dogs, and fewer cats, are clever mole-catchers; but I do not think they eat their prey.

Foxes do eat them on the other hand, so (I have read) do otters; and Gilbert White recorded that a mole-catcher had caught weasels in his traps, so presumably the weasels were hunting moles through the burrows.

Hawks, and particularly buzzards, catch moles when they are working near the surface – their eyes are quick to spot the least movement of the soil.

Hawks are rarer than they used to be; but buzzards are on the whole commoner.

Foxes and weasels might be thought to be eating more moles since myxamatosis has killed off the rabbits.

So we cannot put down the increase in moles to a decline in their natural enemies.

Whatever the cause, we can be quite sure that nature's mysterious sanctions will soon come into operation.

As soon as the moles are too thick on the ground she will send her own particular version of the Four Horsemen of the Apocalypse to spread famine or disease among the moles.

And in two or three years time old countrymen will be saying there have never been so few of the 'little gentlemen in black velvet,' never within man's memory…

We too…

Every biologist knows this will happen. The funny thing is that though we have carefully observed the processes of evolution and natural selection ever since Darwin pointed them out to us, we are curiously unwilling to realise that our species is subject to the same laws.

We, too, are part of nature. Evolution did not cease when man strutted on to the stage. Natural selection applies to us in the long run (though we can put off its operation by various expedients).

Before very long, if we go on breeding too fast, we shall cop it just like the moles.

❖   ❖   ❖

However the ultimate fate of *homo sapiens*, or even the ultimate fate of *talpa europaea* may not immediately concern you if *talpa europaea* happens just now to be burrowing along your row of newly planted peas or beans, or spoiling the look of your lawn.

Trapping is not easy; poisoned worms are dangerous and involve the use of strychnine, which I hope you will never think of buying.

I believe the best bet is carbide of calcium. On a windy day open up the runs of the windward side of your garden and place a few ounces of carbide, slightly moistened, in each.

This may drive the moles off your ground, at any rate. Bad luck on your neighbour!

Skilled

But what we really need are a few good mole-catchers. There used to be one in almost every parish – a chap who would guarantee to rid your whole farm of moles for a pound or two, your garden for the cost of a drink.

He kept and cured the mole-skins, which had an appreciable value. But now they are worthless, and the mole-catcher has almost died out.

He was highly skilled in his curious craft, for trapping moles requires practice, cunning and a good knowledge of their ways.

The Rollright Stones,
Oxfordshire

Apple Trees and a Cuckoo

'*The sweet especial scene*'; the lovely phrase comes from Gerard Manley Hopkins, a poem called *Binsey Poplars,* in which he mourns their being cut down:

> *After-comers cannot guess the beauty been.*
> *Ten or twelve, only ten or twelve*
> *Strokes of havoc unselve*
> *The sweet especial scene.*

How many of us today have known it happen, our 'Sweet especial scene' changed forever, irreparably, by the bulldozer, the mechanical digger, the saw and the axe.

Round about me, it's the apple-orchards which are going. Many of them are old and ruined and worthless today because it's no longer necessary or possible for the farmer to provide his haymakers and harvesters with hundreds of gallons of free cider.

One or two men with a combine harvester can reap and thresh in a day more than a score could do in the old times.

The reapers, working a 12 hour day in the blazing sun, kept themselves going on cider. One hundredth of what they drank would put our combine harvester in the ditch!

So the old and beautiful apple orchards come down. I have witnessed no more breathtaking beauty than that of an orchard with great trees, cider-apple and perry pear, plus a few of the cooking and eating sorts whose names we have long forgotten.

Yet once upon a time such orchards as these made fortunes for their owners.

When I was a young man, in my uncle's auctioneer's office in Tewkesbury we used to hold orchard-sales in early summer the auctioneer walking among the trees the potential bidders following him looking up into the branches to see how the fruit had set.

We offered for sale the crop only; the buyers had to pick and carry it away. I remember seasons when big orchards made hundreds of pounds – a little fortune in those times.

Hardly any

If we go back farther we can read of still greater wealth coming from the boughs of the apple-trees.

According to the records of an old charity: "In 1785 Apples and Pears were remarkably scarce, hardly any grew in the Counties of Worcester, Gloucester and Hereford... What few there were was sold a penny and three ha'pence by the Single Apple."

Most of the orchards must have been barren; but I like to think that here and there a poor man put up his ladders and reaped an unimaginable harvest a penny or three ha'pence in those days when even farthings were counted, for every sound apple picked in the bushel basket hung over his shoulder.

In this early spring I don't mind betting the first of the apple blossom will greet the first cuckoo.

The coincidence of the orchard blossom and the first cuckoo is for me the happiest thing; it never fails to lift my heart.

If in this season I can go among my old, decaying, useless but still lovely apple-trees, and see the pink and white blossom opening on them, and hear the cuckoo at the same time, I shall be contented.

When you're in your fifties you begin to count up your springs.

The herald

Every year nowadays I long for the cuckoo. His voice for me is the herald of the real spring. Up till then we've had snowdrops, crocuses, daffodils, celandines.

Now at last we get the greenness and the gold and the whiteness and the cream, the whole cornucopia prodigally poured out.

I think the cuckoo is wise to leave us when he does. Matthew Arnold in *Thyrsis* cried out to him:

Too quick despairer wherefore wilt thou go?
Soon will the high Midsummer pomps come on;...

But if I were a cuckoo I think I'd like to remember England by its springs and not by its midsummer pomps of heavy-scented flowers mostly purple and red, which belongs to the months after the last cuckoo has left us.

New-laundered

The pomps of summer are splendid, I know; but give me the yellow and the green and the new-laundered white of the flowers which bloom when the first cuckoo calls.

I'll be listening hard for him this year, from April the twelfth to the fifteenth.

Wessex Saddleback

On Keeping Cats and Birds

This is the time of the year when I begin to suffer from a sort of split-mind on the subject of cats and garden birds. I love both; which is like trying to have one's cake and eat it, or, shall I say, to have one's cat and let it eat them.

Up to a point, however, cats and birds are not mutually exclusive. The resident feline population of our garden and orchard is two Siamese and three ordinary cats: 2.5 to the acre. Despite this we harbour two pairs of robins, one each of thrushes, blackbirds, and chaffinches, numberless house-sparrows, and in summer a pair of spotted fly-catchers. All these nest with us.

On the other hand I have got to admit that there are occasional tragedies. Scarlett, the tortoiseshell, climbing up the creeper, had the young spotted fly-catchers one summer, but the birds have returned and bred safely since.

❈   ❈   ❈

The big black cat, Candy, is a rabbiter who doesn't often trouble her head about birds, but when she does so she is curiously selective, a serious student, it appears, of the science of ornithology, for she is apt to lay a greenfinch proudly at the back door, or some scarce visitor like a siskin or a twite, which we only see once in two or three years. If a hoopoe descended on our lawn, Candy would have it; yet she is on excellent terms with the robins, who hop about within a few feet of me while I am digging, watched by Candy with her yellow contemplative eyes. I think they tease her, like the canary who taut she taw a Puddy Tat; and the old cat has at last discovered that they are under my protection and that it is best to take no notice of them.

For the rest, Floosie, the long-haired tabby, is too stupid to catch anything, and is chiefly interested in admiring her own beautiful tail; whereas the Siamese are games-players rather than hunters, who spend hours dribbling a ping-pong ball and passing it to and fro like inside forwards practising for the Cup tie.

So you see it is possible for cats and birds to share the garden; and the cats certainly help in the summer to frighten the blackbirds off the strawberries, thus making up to me for the way they kick up the fine tilth of the seedbeds in the spring. (For this reason none of my flowers or vegetables grow in neat rows or regular patterns; the lines of lettuces and carrots have a kink in them every few yards where one of the cats scratched out her little hole at planting time. The seeds come up all the same, like toadstools in a fairy-ring; and my gardener, who is unique among his kind in liking cats, only smiles tolerantly and says 'That was our Candy that was!'

※　　※　　※

But, seriously, if you want to keep cats without sacrificing your birds there are several things you can do about it. You can make, or buy, cat-poof nesting boxes, and they will afford complete protection for those species which use them. You can refrain from feeding your birds *on the ground*, especially in hard weather (for if you do so the cats will think you are baiting a trap for their benefit, and act accordingly). Therefore, design yourself a bird-table which cats can't climb on to. It is wise, in any case, to avoid making your birds too tame if you keep cats; for thus you thoughtlessly betray them. Robins are the exception to this rule. However tame they become, their little beady eyes are on the look-out, and they can be trusted to look after themselves.

Finally – and this is the most important point of all – see that your cats are well fed. If you subscribe to the theory that in order to be a good mouser a cat must be half starved, then you can not expect the birds to share your garden with it; for hunger does not differentiate between feather and fur.

※　　※　　※

Mr. E.M. Nicholson, the author of *Birds and Men*, quotes some interesting estimates of the cat population of Britain. The

British Institute of Public Opinion (heaven knows why) tried to find out how many cats there were in the County of London, and decided that there were half a million; whereas in Britain as a whole, according to the National Animal Registration Service, there are no less than fourteen million. If this figure is correct it means that there are more cats than any individual species of bird! For our commonest birds, the chaffinch and the blackbird, are each only ten millions strong; whereas there are but seven million each of robins and starlings, and house sparrows, song thrushes and meadow pipits not more than three million each.

If I were a house-sparrow I think I should be very alarmed at the thought of being out-numbered by cats to the tune of nearly three to one! And apparently there are eleven cats to every wren, nineteen to every linnet, and forty-two to every greenfinch; so it seems little short of miraculous that the songsters survive at all, especially as they have to contend with rats, weasels, predatory birds, grey squirrels and boys, all of which steal their eggs or nestlings. The only conclusion I can draw from these figures is that cats do much less harm to the birds than they are supposed to; for there are probably less than 100 million birds (including large ones) in Britain altogether, so if every cat ate 7.14 birds in a year there would be no birds left!

(N.B.; I have taken the estimates of bird populations from Mr. James Fisher's excellent *Watching Birds* in the Pelican Books series.)

When St. David's Men wore a Lily

The lily that good Welshmen used to wear in their button-holes and caps on this Saint David's Day commemorates their victory over the Saxons in the year 640.

The story goes that St. David, in addition to praying that the Welsh might win, made a practical suggestion towards that end.

Since neither side, of course, wore any uniforms, it was always difficult to know which of two barbarians was which. Let the Welsh, therefore, wear a distinguishing badge – and what more apt and suitable emblem than –

A *lily*, did I say? Surely I meant a leek? But a leek *is* a lily, though Pistol, whom Fluellen invited to eat one in *King Henry V*, would hardly have agreed.

"Not for Cadwallader and all his goats!" said he; for he was "qualmish," as he put it, "at the smell of leek."

However, with the aid of a cudgel, Fluellen compelled him to swallow one. "If you can mock a leek you can eat a leek. It is good for your green wound and your bloody coxcomb..." and so on.

Cousins

Pistol would have had something remarkable to say about it if somebody had told him that he was devouring a lily.

But the leek belongs to the genus *Allium*, which comprises also the onion, shallot and the garlic. This genus in turn belongs to the *Liliacae*, so that the leek's more attractive cousins include the little blue Scilla which brightens the spring, the Lily of the Valley, the Hyacinth and the Tulip. The Asphodel, the Star of Bethlehem, and of course, those "lilies of the field" mentioned in the Sermon on the Mount, the Scarlet Turk's Cap, *Lilium Chalcedicum,* which paints the Syrian plains blood-red.

❀　❀　❀

We English no longer have Pistol's prejudice against leeks.

Nor do we have any inhibition about the eating of onions. Any noontide in my local you are liable to see half-a-dozen hefty fellows, who have been working hard in the fields all the morning, settle down to their bait, which consists of hunks of bread and butter with cold bacon or cold meat, and one or two large raw onions.

They eat them as you would an apple, a good big bite at a time; between mouthfuls they sip their cider.

Since they devour raw onions almost every day of their lives except Sundays, they are connoisseurs in this respect – some years the onions are better than others, certain strains have a better flavour, onions grown from seed (some hold) taste better than those grown from sets.

I doubt if this is true, incidentally; but we have some old chaps who are curiously prejudiced against sets, which are an easy way of growing onions – for one thing you don't have to hobble along bent double as you try to sprinkle seeds not much bigger than specks of dust evenly into a drill.

The old chaps, having done this all their lives, don't like to think of the younger ones having it easy,

"They're frit o' the backache nowadays," they say. "They're shy of hard work."

Good things, they reason, can only be had by taking pains. The more backache, the better onions. Therefore the little bulbs or sets, which you simply press into the ground at the right intervals, no thinning out, no difficult weeding – they make gardening too simple. There must be a catch in it somewhere!

※　　※　　※

Our attitude to garlic is very strange indeed. Only a sophisticated minority of English people use it for cooking; not one in a thousand, I imagine, grows it in his garden.

I do, as is happens, and jolly useful it is. But these fellows who think nothing of eating at one meal two raw onions each as big as a cricket ball, look upon the faintest flavour of garlic as a kind of foreign wickedness.

Puritanism

Somehow or other I think our English puritanism is involved. We associate garlic with Italian extravagances and French goings-on.

"You just ought to *smell* 'em," says one of our bait-eaters, much travelled by reason of his service in two wars.

"Blimey, 'nuff to knock you down!"

And leaning towards you he breathes an honest English exhalation of onion right into your face.

Tithe Barn at Bredon

If we have a March Blossom

The wild daffodils, or Lent Lilies, as some folk call them, are coming out already in their favourite damp places along the valleys between the hills.

I have heard country people call them affodils, which is interesting because the word daffodil is a corruption of asphodel. How gaily they dance in a March wind!

However cold the spring or late the season, they beat the swallows to it, as Shakespeare well knew, these 'daffodils that come before the swallow dares.'

So do the celandines, those shiniest of spring flowers. Their yellow petals look as if they had been polished, then painted with one of those transparent varnishes.

Never a March goes by but we find them in bloom along the hedge-bank.

Swallow

But they should match the swallows coming – according to their name. Greek *khelidon* means swallow; hence celandine, the swallow-flower.

But as a rule, the celandines are nearly over by the time the swallows arrive; the Sweet Pilgrims, as one of the minor Elizabethan poets sweetly called them.

His name was Sir Henry Wooton and he was a friend of Izaak Walton...

> *There stood my Friend with patient Skill*
> *Attending of his trembling Quill,*

wrote he,

> *Already were the Eaves possesst*
> *With the Sweet Pilgrim's daubed nest.*

That charming and natural little poem ends with the lines:

All looked gay, and full of Cheer
To welcome the New-livered Year

Shiny

Daffs and celandines, lady-smocks, primroses, violets and kingcups will weave themselves in the pattern of that livery very soon.

Did I say that the celandine was the shiniest of flowers?

Then I had forgotten those kingcups, or marsh-marigolds, 'cuckoo-buds of yellow hue,' Shakespeare called them.

They shine so bright you might expect to see your face in them. (You can't though. Their faces on a sunny day are reflected in yours as all the buttercups' are. Do you remember how when you were a child you held a buttercup up to some-one's chin in the spring sunshine, and said; 'do you like butter?' And the yellow was reflected on their chin, and, of course, they did like butter – who doesn't?)

Yellow

So many of the early-spring flowers are yellow that it seems to be the season's hue... crocus, celandine, kingcup, and buttercup, coltsfoot, dandelion, daffodil, and so on.

But upon the boughs spring comes in white first upon the blackthorn, whose frail petals make the thinnest snow upon twigs which are ebon at this time of year.

The sprinkling is so slight, the little flowers look so precarious and tender, that there is something touching, almost pitiful, about the sight of a blackthorn bush standing in the teeth of a March nor'easter.

First

This wildling is the very first of the plums. When its wan flowers open we know that the orchards won't be very slow to follow suit.

Sometimes it is only a fortnight or so between the first blackthorn blooms and the lace-curtain loveliness on the Prolifics and Pershores in the Evesham Vale.

Given a very mild month, with some soft winds and warm sun during the last fortnight, we might get a March blossom which happens perhaps one year in five or six.

If it happens this year, it will be an Easter blossom, too; and March 29, Easter Day, will perhaps be Blossom Sunday.

The Bell Hotel,
Tewkesbury

The Man who thinks like a Hawk

Hawks and falcons are beautiful and terrible, the most savage, uncompromising and tameless of wild things.

'Tameless?' you ask with surprise – remembering old pictures of the hooded hawk on its owner's wrist.

It is true that you can break the spirit of the bird through a combination of hunger and lack of sleep; in much the same way as Petruchio subdued Katherine.

Indeed, 'The Taming the Shrew' would serve quite well as a text on falconry.

But I do not believe the falconer ever really *possesses* the beautiful creature that he 'tames' to be his slave, the wild spirit within it is ever crying to be free.

For my part I would not wish to possess or to master one; I'd say to myself like Othello:

Though that her jesses were my dear heart-strings
I'd whistle her off and let her down the wind
To prey at fortune...

Awe-inspiring

These birds have always caught the imagination of poets. The 'stoop' of a falcon, his dive upon his prey, is one of the most awe-inspiring sights in nature.

There are some magnificent descriptions of it in a new book by a new writer, 'The Peregrine' by J. A. Baker, (Collins, 25s).

Mr Baker spent 10 winters watching peregrines in East Anglia.

Whenever he found one which had established itself in a particular hunting-ground he became, as it were, its shadow, its doppelganger, its ever-watchful sleuth; 'Wherever he goes this winter I will follow him', he writes. 'I will share the fear, and the exaltation and the boredom of his hunting life.'

A bond

Before long Mr. Baker was conscious of 'an extraordinary bond between watcher and watched.'

He did indeed 'share' with the falcon its weariness, hunger, disappointment and frustrations – and of course the terrible triumph of the ultimate kill.

The bird, though always suspicious, became used to the fact that for long days on end this man was never out of sight.

The victims

Identifying himself so closely with the bird the man got to know its habits in every small detail; how it searched for its prey, what it looked for, even what it saw through those magnificent hawk-eyes.

During 10 winters he witnessed or found the remains of 619 kills.

He gives an interesting list of the birds involved – 45 species, woodpigeons and black-headed gulls being the principal victims.

But while he was watching the peregrines, Mr. Baker's sharp eyes took in the whole of the natural scene.

He describes every incident superbly; indeed his book is something quite exceptional in the way of nature writing; Gilbert White himself would have admired it, and I'm sure W. H. Hudson never did anything as good.

He describes, for instance, the golden plover rising 'like puffs of gunsmoke' and you say to yourself, if you've ever watched a golden plover 'Yes, it's exactly like that, why on earth didn't I think of that phrase!'

And here's a fieldmouse feeding on a slope of grass: 'His long delicate ears were like hands unfolding; his huge, night-seeing eyes were opaque and dark.

'He was unaware of my face a foot above him. I was like a galaxy to him, too big to be seen.'

Beautiful...

A poet wrote those lines. But back to the peregrines.

Their world – which this tireless watcher came nearer to knowing than any man has done before – is that of the hunter and the hunted; even weather and landscape are only relevant in so far as they affect the urgencies of slaughter or escape from slaughter.

It's a world of death and blood in which pity, in the ordinary sense, has no place; 'The striving of birds to kill or to save themselves from death, is beautiful to see.'

If you do not believe this then let me quote you a few sentences from this superb account of a peregrine's stoop upon a partridge. The falcon had dived at a steepening angle from a thousand feet or more.

Shimmering

'He had another thousand feet to fall, but he fell sheer, shimmering down through dazzling sunlight heart-shaped, like a heart in flames...'

'The partridge in the snow beneath looked up at the black heart dilating down upon him and heard a hiss of wings rising to a roar.

'In 10 seconds the hawk was down and the whole splendid fabric, the arched reredos and immense fan-vaulting of his flight was consumed and lost in the fiery maelstrom of the sky.

'And for the partridge there was the sun suddenly shut out, the roar ceasing, the blazing knives driving in, the terrible white face descending – hooked and masked and horned and staring-eyed.

'And then... snow scattering from scuffling feet, and snow filling the bill's wide silent scream...'

When Women take Command

I had an encounter the other day which reminded me painfully of the last war and filled me with apprehension about the next. And yet I suppose she was really a very nice girl, well brought-up, good mannered, capable, tidy-minded, the sort of whom her headmistress in her last-term report writes enthusiastically: 'Phyllis made an excellent Captain of the School and of the Hockey XI. She is a born leader.'

Sitting opposite her in the railway carriage, I wondered why she filled me with such deep despair.

She was a Junior Commander in the A.T.S.; and she was talking about the latest batch of recruits which had come under her for training. "You wouldn't believe," she said, "what an assorted mess they look when they first arrive. All daubed with make-up" – her own was of the discreetest – "and some of them with long hair hanging down their backs like Lauren Bacall!"

'Does that matter?' I said, to tease her; and she looked appropriately shocked.

'Of course it does. They couldn't tuck it up under their caps, you see.'

※　※　※

It was then that I recognised the thing which all my life, wherever I have met it, has most depressed me; the Military Mind. For one of its principle characteristics is that it somehow identifies virtue with short hair (just as the contemporaries of Samson identified it with long hair). It likes to see the pinky-white scalp showing through the close-cropped stubble at the back of a man's head; and what is worse, it identifies virtue with conformity, without understanding that that is exactly what Hitler did.

'Moore, why was Able-Seaman Jones absent from church parade?'

'Seventh Day Adventist, sir.'
'And you yourself?'
'Agnostic, sir,'
'Are you sure you're *allowed* to be an Agnostic in the Royal Navy?'

※　　※　　※

The Military Mind is bad enough in a man; but, oh my hat, it is a terrifying thing in a woman! For women; however nice, are apt to enjoy tormenting other women; and military authority gives them exceptional opportunities to do so. For most of the war, for instance, girls in the services were not allowed to carry handbags; nor were they allowed to fill their pocket with oddments which made them bulge. Naturally this was sheer torture to the poor girls; for our local Women's Institute played a game the other day in which everybody had to turn out their handbags and count the individual items they contained. The average number of items was 33; the winner had nearly a hundred, not counting coins and stamps.

When I was married, in 1944, my wife, who was a Wren, and in uniform, wore a bag hung on a strap over the shoulder. A photograph appeared in the evening paper which just showed the strap of the bag. When she returned to her camp two days later she was on the mat before the Wren Officer;

'Moore' – she hardly recognised the name as belonging to her – 'Wren Moore, have you seen this photograph? Why were you wearing a shoulder-bag contrary to regulations at your wedding?'

※　　※　　※

If war comes again, most of us will go back, hating it but accepting the necessary duty, the danger, the frustration and above all the unutterable boredom as we did before. But I suppose it is too much to hope that to all these miseries will not be super-added the Military Mind, which loves uniformity and hates individuality and has one ambition greater even than the ambition to win – to press us all into a common mould?

Does it really make us better soldiers and sailors if we crop our hair like convicts? Do girls make better A.T.S. and airwomen if they 'turn it up under their caps?' Do Wrens make better typists or mess waitresses if we teach them to march and form threes and compel them to attend a time-wasting parade twice a week? I cannot believe it.

❊   ❊   ❊

And that is why the nice girl in the train filled me with despair. She reminded me of Mrs. Warren's daughter in the play, indeed of almost all Shaw's heroines except Saint Joan, with their prim orderly minds and their perpetual desire to organise people.

I do not for a moment suggest that they like war; but it gives them their opportunity for they are said to be 'officer types'. One again, I do not believe it. To my mind, an 'officer type' is wise, humane, humorous and tolerant, and being chosen for individuality should recognise that quality in others. Nelson was such a one; and you don't discover your Nelsons if you try to cast everybody in the same mould.

King John Bridge,
Tewkesbury

On being Eleven – A Reverie

The first sound is so slight – it is the faintest imaginable flip – that only by reason of my misspent youth do I immediately recognise its import. The second sound, right over my head is a very distinct *whoo-oo-sh* followed by a brief rustle in the boughs of the apple-tree which leans over my garden-wall. Some torn-off leaves come tumbling down; but fortunately there are no feathers. A faintly-puzzled cock blackbird breaks off his singing and leisurely flies away.

He is luckier than he knows; for when, sallying out, I pounce upon the tow-headed eleven-year-old I discover that the weapon was fairly lethal; there are seven, no, nine notches on the handles. The prong is cut from a stout hazel – we used to shape ours out of the tops of cigar-boxes, of which I can still recollect the aromatic smell; but, of course, cigar-boxes are rarer today.

The elastic is of the square-sided black sort, somewhat like liquorice and apt to be confused with liquorice if it has inhabited a sticky pocket for a few weeks. There were other kinds of elastic which were offered to us by shopkeepers lacking in understanding; we scorned them, holding them to be fit only for girls' garters, and always insisted that the only true catty-lacky was the square-sided, costing, in those days, twopence-ha'penny a yard.

❀   ❀   ❀

The ends of this excellent elastic (I now notice with an appraising eye) are neatly compressed through grooves nicked into the top of each prong, the prongs then being whipped with waxed string. The sling itself is made of chamois-leather, which is very superior and professional; we used to cut the tongues out of old and not-so-old shoes. The notches on the handle are of different sizes, and this, I fear, may have some dark significance. I resolve not to enquire into it.

Instead I discourse upon the sacrosanct nature of blackbirds in the breeding season. The tow-headed urchin stares at me with a resentful and defensive stare which uncomfortably reminds me of my own expression some 35 years ago. Do I confiscate the catapult, thus saving, perhaps, the lives of a few beloved songsters? I recollect my hatred, almost murderous, of one such confiscator, and I realise that I am not really cut out for the role.

I, therefore, hand back the weapon and recommend target-practice on tins. I know quite well, however, that no normal boy – and this one is aggressively normal – will get any satisfaction out of target-practice on tins. The normal boy requires a living target; he requires, to put it brutally, to see the feathers fly. Such a spectacle nowadays causes me deep distress; but then I am no longer eleven.

❂   ❂   ❂

Catapults are better than coshes, I reassure myself; though on reflection I am not sure that they are less murderous. The word is Greek for 'to hurl against,' and a well-made catty can hurl a round pebble from the brook against Goliath or any other sizeable target with extraordinary force.

Gypsies use catapults in their gang-warfare, and I know one Cyclopian fellow called Black Alfred who lost his left eye by reason of his opponent's good marksmanship. Moreover it is not necessary to use a stone; a bullet is better and in my youth I possessed a device like a pair of forceps with hollow and rounded ends which fitted tightly together and had a small hole in the top into which one could force molten lead.

The molten lead was usually an ex-Highlander, Uhlan, Dragoon or Horse Guard broken off his stand in the course of some skirmish of the toy soldiers. He was poured into the curious instrument – can it have been made for this purpose? – out of which when, when the lead had cooled, came a heavy, round bullet. This was deadlier than any pebble.

❂   ❂   ❂

I made a score of such bullets in readiness for the arrival of the so-called Garden Gun which I'd seen advertised in some boys' paper about the time of my tenth birthday. **NO LICENCE REQUIRED,** said the advertisement, **SHOOTS ACCURATELY WITH STONES OR LEAD PELLETS.**

Alas, when the Garden Gun arrived it consisted simply of an ash walking stick, not quite straight, into one end of which was screwed a metal prong; at the other end was a kind of trigger and a clip into which the sling of a catapult could be fitted. The elastic, of course, was tied to the ends of the metal prong. I had little faith in the weapon, and less faith after I had fired it, because it was the only gun I have ever owned which could shoot round corners.

The first experimental discharge, aimed at a post at the bottom of the garden, produced a neat round hole in a shirt which hung upon a neighbour's clothes-line, in the garden which ran parallel with ours. The second produced a tinkling of glass which I did not wait to investigate. **SHOOTS ACCURATELY WITH LEAD PELLETS...**

I ran into the house, and hid, and nursed my first bitter disillusion about the integrity of advertisers. The Garden Gun found its way into the junk room among the jigsaw puzzles which had the most important pieces missing, and the clockwork toys that had broken their mainsprings, and the Teddy Bear that used to grunt when one pressed his tummy, but had lost his grunt when I was about seven.

Why Nancy had Indigestion

The Rev. James Woodforde, of whom I wrote in this column the other day, kept a diary from the year 1758 until he died in 1802.

Since he was extremely fond of his food and drink, and wrote down in detail what he had for dinner almost every day, he gives us a very good idea of the kind of meals which fairly well-off country folk enjoyed during the latter part of the 18th century.

Swell occasion

I find this altogether fascinating. The first thing that strikes you is how much they ate:

'*Sept. 24, 1790: Nancy (his niece) was taken very ill this Afternoon with a pain within her, blown up so as if poisoned, attended with a vomiting.*

'*I supposed it proceeded in great measure from what she ate at Dinner and afterwards: some boiled Beef rather fat and salt, a good deal of roast duck and a plenty of boiled Damson Pudding.*

'*After Dinner by way of Desert she ate some greengage Plumbs, some Figgs, and raspberries and Cream... Going to bed I gave her a good dose of Rhubarb and Ginger.*

'*Sept. 25: Nancy Thank God Much better this Morning – the Rhubarb made her rise earlier than usual. She dined on a rost Neck of Mutton...*'

Here is an example of a Bill of Fare for a rather swell occasion in January:

'*First Course Cod and Oyster Sauce, Roast Beef, tongue and boiled Chicken, Peas (presumably dried), Soups and Roots.*

'*Second course a Turkey, a brace of Partridge rosted, Snipes and some Larks rosted, also an Orange Pudding, syllabubs and Jellies, Madeira and Port Wine to drink and a dish of Fruit...*'

'Dinner' happened in the afternoon, generally about 2.30. It often went on for two or three hours. I imagine there was a longish interval between the First Course and the Second Course, to give you time to get your second wind!

Most of the dishes sound much the same as good plain country cooking today; though in the winter, game of various kinds largely took the place of 'butcher's meat', and His reverence was apt to dine off snipe, teal, mallard, widgeon, woodcock, partridge, pheasant and hare.

Tewkesbury Abbey

He sometimes had 'whistling plover' – that is golden plover, which I have sometimes shot in Wales.

It is delicious – almost as good as partridge. In those days long before any Wild Bird's Protection Act, the sameness of one's winter diet was often relieved by larks, thrushes, fieldfares and even a Nursery Rhyme 'Blackbird Pie.'

Coarse fish were important; those from the sea were apt to be rather high before they arrived at your home save in the coldest weather.

Mr Woodforde enjoyed carp, tench, perch, fried dace, eels done in a variety of ways, pike (cooked generally á la Izaak Walton, with 'a pudding in his belly'); even gudgeons were not despised.

Salmon cost 9d a pound; the best tea, on the other hand, cost at least 12s a pound. The comparative costs of those two commodities are very different nowadays!

Puddings comprised blancmanges, custards, syllabubs, pies, fritters, jellies and all manner of 'dumplings', which doubtless contributed to the Parson's indigestion, which looms so largely in his Diary that the 5-volume edition includes **INDIGESTION** in the Index – with about a dozen entries in some of the volumes!

When he went out to dinner he wasn't always pleased with what he was given;

'Some salt Fish, with Eggs in their Shells, Potatoes and turnips, a Hare spoiled in rosting, some Parts much over done, others scarce hot thro', with their Head taken off, and laid on each side of the Dish; also a Pudding made of Cranberries in a large white Basin.

'The Paste very ordinary I think. I cannot say I made a very good Dinner'.

Blacksmiths Ancient and Modern

Oh the sizzling, the stamping, the hot-iron smells and the burnt-hoof smells, the sparks that flew like little shooting-stars, in the dim-dark smithy in the days of my youth!

Next to the taxidermist's shop in the neighbouring town, where there were stuffed owls and otters, boxes of glass eyes, tropical butterflies, fearful scalpels and strong whiffs of naphthalene, the blacksmith's was the most exciting establishment I knew.

Everybody is romantic about blacksmiths; there's Longfellow's hackneyed poem and Gerard Manley Hopkins' grand one – he wrote it, you'll remember, to a farrier who had lost his strength, and pined, and sickened, and died –

> *Poor Felix Randal,*
> *How far from then forethought of, all thy more*
>   *boisterous years,*
> *When thou at the random grim forge, powerful*
>   *amidst peers,*
> *Didst fettle for the great grey drayhorse his bright*
>   *and battering sandal!*

The blacksmith who caught my imagination when I was a child, was called, not very appositely, Mr. White.

Drayhorses

He shod, not only hunters, but the drayhorses of the Midland Railway and the shaggy-fetlocked Shire horses.

And the huge Suffolk Punches that drew the farm wagons at haytime and harvest and ploughed the fields in winter, heaving hoofs bigger than dinner plates step by step with the sticky soil upon them, as they plodded their eight miles of hard-going in the course of a seven-hour day to plough three roods of ground with a nine-inch furrow.

In my memory they are splendid and stupid, patient most of the time but liable to sudden panics not knowing their own strength.

Mr. White's muscles really did stand out like iron bands when he lifted their hind hooves, gripped them between his knees and hammered in the nails to secure the 'bright and battering sandal.'

Long talks

When I was old enough to have a hunter I took it to be shod by Mr. White and got to know him well enough to have some long talks while the job was done.

He claimed that as a Sergeant Farrier in the Boer War he had shod for Winston Churchill the horse on which he escaped from his brief captivity by the Boers.

But Mr. White was gloomy about the prospects for his trade; "I be the last on 'em. There wun't be any more, hereabouts. The world's changing, and they've no use for we any more."

Fat ponies

He was utterly mistaken. The Suffolk Punches and the great grey drayhorses have disappeared but there are still the hunters – at least as many as there were in 1939 – the flourishing pony clubs, with their innumerable fat Thelwell ponies and their countless pony-mad Thelwell schoolgirls.

There are pony-trekkers in the hill-country, there are the riding schools and of course the point-to-points, the training stables and the races still.

In fact, I daresay there are more horses, within say, a 20-mile radius of my house than there were in the late Thirties.

The social levelling-down and levelling-up has meant, as it was bound to do, that more and more people can afford ponies for their children.

And why not? This seems to me the most agreeable aspect of socialism; that more people can afford the sort of fun which I, as a moderately 'privileged' country boy, enjoyed in my childhood.

Likewise, more adults can afford to go to riding-schools, take part in pony-treks, even to hunt foxes. Only people with chips on their shoulders can object to this.

In demand

Meanwhile the blacksmith, whose job is now diversified by the demand for quick repair of farm machinery and for the manufacture of arty wrought-ironwork for newcomers to the countryside, is more in demand than ever he was before.

Few of us nowadays take our horse to his forge; he shoes them as I learnt to do myself years and years ago when I was a Territorial soldier, by cold shoeing.

He comes along with his assistant in a small van and brings with him some suitable shoes for the particular horses we have asked him to shoe that day.

He keeps in his mind, as all blacksmiths should, a clear picture of the feet of his regular customers.

Especially he remembers if there is anything unusual; a slight malformation, a tendency to over-reach, a foot which needs building up a little with an extra-thick shoe.

So when we ring up and say 'Zena needs two hind shoes, Skipper wants shoeing all round, Nou-Nou's O.K. except for her near-fore,' he either takes the necessary shoes from his stock or makes them specially in his forge and brings them with him on whichever day of the week he visits our neighbourhood.

Then he trims and pares the hooves and fits the shoes as accurately, I'm sure, as Felix Randal did in his 'random grim forge' where the hooves sizzled and the sharp smoke from it tickled everybody's noses and the bellows blew and the furnace blazed and the sparks flew like shooting stars.

Kozikot or No. 99?

They who would like it if they could to number us all, so that John Smith would become XYZ/H2.6789 – they who strove so hard, when the war was finished and done with, to fasten utterly useless Identity Cards bearing some such code-numbers upon John Smith and you and me for ever – they who hate anything individual, personal, unhandy-to-pigeonhole, are now turning their attention to the names of our dwellings.

Kozikot, Ivydene, Resthaven, Lime Villa are perhaps not very original or attractive names; but for the habitations of free people they are a jolly sight better than Numbers 54, 55, 56 and 57. Cowstalls may be numbered so; or pigsties; or lock-up garages. But to my mind even the meanest two-up and two-downer, even the most jerrybuilt box of bricks which enshrines the hearth and the household goods of Mr. John Smith deserves the dignity of a name.

Town Councils do not think so. They not only see to it that the Units, as they call them, on the New Housing Estate, are numbered instead of named, but wherever there is a row of older houses upon which past occupants have exercised their fancy in this matter of names, the Local Authority delights to abolish the names and substitute numbers.

I don't say they all do so, but it seems to be a current bureaucratic craze. If you ask why, they will tell you that it makes things easier for various people – clerks and rate-collectors and postmen. But if you were a postman wouldn't you prefer to deliver this, even if the handwriting *were* a bit squiggly;

John Smith Esq.,
　Blighty,
　　Lilliput Lane,
　　　Tiddleytown.

than
> John Smith Esq.,
>   177, New Estate West,
>   Tiddleytown - ?

❋   ❋   ❋

Because even the squiggliest 'Blighty' is hardly liable to be confused with even the most spidery 'Kozikot' where, of course, another John Smith has his habitation; whereas quite a lot of people write their 'sevens' like 'fours' (all Continental people do) and some careless folk make them like 'nines' (especially old Auntie Jane, who's eyesight is failing a little as she approaches ninety). so that Christmas letter from that *eine kleine* Fraulein whom John Smith met when he was with the Army of Occupation, goes to the John Smith who lives at 144; because, of course, the *eine kleine* Fraulein crosses the tops of her sevens.

And the woollen scarf which Auntie Jane knitted for her nephew goes to the John Smith who lives at 199. He has no Aunt Jane, but he collars the scarf, and Auntie, receiving no letter of thanks from nephew John, does not after all leave him a thousand pounds.

Well, it could happen, couldn't it? So I don't mind betting that the postman, if he were asked, would just as soon have names as numbers. In any case I am sure that postmen are proud and splendid and honourable men, fully aware of human dignities, and that they are the last people in the world to wish to turn Mr. Smith's cosy little 'Blighty' into Number 177.

❋   ❋   ❋

Even if this is not so, let me point out that these admirable postmen have been delivering letters to houses with names, with the minimum of error, for precisely 114 years. They started to do so when the envelopes had black penny stamps, without perforations, bearing the head of a young queen. I do not believe that the postmen whose letters bear tuppeny-ha'penny stamps, bearing the head of another young queen, are any less intelligent than their Victorian predecessors. They are probably more so.

So why the insistence upon numbers? I'll make a guess. It is for the trifling convenience of pettifogging little clerks in offices who keep files. And although it is perfectly easy to card-index files under a system of names, as every business man knows these little chaps love numbers. They love XYZ/H2/6789, not for any reason of aesthetics or convenience, but simply because it makes them feel official and important.

❊   ❊   ❊

If they were dealing with a file marked 'Blighty' or 'Kozikot' they would feel unofficial and not half so important; but they might, perhaps, feel more human, mightn't they? They might even begin to wonder what sort of a fellow was this John Smith, living at 'Blighty'.

And wondering so, they might think of him as a real person instead of an XYZ; and when he made an application to keep angora rabbits in his back garden, or build a little shed to accommodate his model railway, they might even smile to themselves and write 'Application granted' on his file.

And that would never do, would it?

Country Causerie

Those beshorted and rucksack-burdened walkers who insist on describing themselves as hikers sometimes seem to imagine that they are doing something original; to forget, in fact, that mankind's natural method of progression is upon his two legs. I read that a Hiking Club's Easter excursion, lasting three days, will involve a journey on foot of "more than forty miles"; and this is presented as an interesting item of news.

Would it be fair to remind the Hiking Club that in the year 1618 Ben Jonson being then aged 46 *walked from London to Edinburgh* to visit a friend there? On the way he drank as much ale, sack and canary as would have sunk half a dozen Hikers' Clubs; and arriving at the house of his friend and fellow-poet, Drummond of Hawthornden, he practically drank his cellar dry, so that Drummond observed sombrely when the great man had taken his departure, "Drink is one of the elements he lives in."

A vapour

I love Eric Linklater's description of Rare Ben Jonson setting out upon his journey on a hot summer's day; "He must have larded the lean earth like Falstaff, watered the ground in knots like Dame Ursula. Like Chaucer's Canon, it must have been 'joye for to seen him swete'. A vapour would rise from him, canary-scented, pearly as evening mist sun-drawn out of fat meadows, and down his neck, down his great chest and the vastness of his back would tumble a hundred streams to part in diverging floods to either side of his noble belly and (drawing tributaries from that many-fountained Ida) wash faster to his knees."

Toast him, you 40 mile Hikers, as you sip your half-pints of lemonade shandy and nibble your lettuce sandwiches in the bar.

Kipling's herbs

Some little time back I wrote in this column of cottage-garden herbs and their ancient, sweet and curious names, such as Bergamot and Pennyroyal. A correspondent now reminds me of some even prettier names enshrined in a poem by Kipling called "Our Fathers of Old."

> *Excellent herbs had our fathers of old*
> *Excellent herbs to ease their pain –*
> *Alexanders and Marigold,*
> *Eyebright, Orris and Elecampane,*
> *Basil, Rocket, Valerian, Rue,*
> *(Almost singing themselves they run)*
> *Vervain, Dittany, Call-me-to-you,*
> *Cowslip, Melilot, Rose-of-the-Sun.*

Can anyone tell me what flower it is that was known as "Call-me-to-you" by our fathers of old? I delight in these many-hyphenated names of flowers, for instance, Jack-go-to-bed-at-noon for the Goatsbeard, and Welcome-your-husband-whether-he-come-home-drunk-or-nay, a piece of humane advice which also serves, in Somerset, for the name of a plant called the Biting Stonecrop.

Pussy willow

And every year, at this season, the name Pussy Willow pleases me afresh. We call them Sallies too – the sedate botanists say Sallows – but this is when they are fully out, gold-dusted, "mealed-with-yellow" as Gerard Manley Hopkins put it in a poem.

The Pussies, I think, are the flowers before they fully open, when they are silver-grey and furry, like short-haired Persians. Children stroke them then, finding a strange joy in their soft furriness. But it only takes two or three days of sun to turn them from silver to gold; and then the pollen-smeared bees get busy about them buzzing all day long, sucking the sweetness only half-recollected during winter's long dream.

The humming ceases at dusk, and then come the moths, especially those drab ones which our fathers of old called Quakers because of their modest dress. They hang on to the sally-blossom until they are drunk with its honey; and if you shine a torch upon the sally-bushes then you will see a multitude of little red eyes, reflecting the torchlight, many-faceted miniatures of those cats-eyes which provident County Councils sink into the tarmac of our roads.

Lych gate at Long Compton,
Warwickshire

Elm may hate Man but...

One of the grimmest country sayings I know runs like this:

Elm hateth
Man, and waiteth.

Some say the meaning is that the tree will sometimes treacherously, even in calm weather, 'drop a limb on the head of him who doubteth her sovereign will.'

But I think the implication behind the rhyme is really to do with coffins, which are largely made of elm.

But if elm hateth man, this man loveth the elm. I love the shape of the tree, a sort of superb untidiness, which mocks the petty orderliness of suburban housing estates in which by some rare act of tolerance the last of the field elms is permitted to remain.

I love the wine-red tint when the flowers come on the bare branches where the noisy rooks like black blobs caw about their windy nests; all March epitomised in such a scene.

I love the soft green of the little leaves which come as a rule in late April, so that country boys have a saying, 'when the leaves on the ellums is no bigger'n mouse's ears, that's the season for love.'

Magnificent

Elms in high summer, brooding magnificent trees, with woodpigeons invisible among the leafage – 'coo of doves in immemorial elms.'

In autumn, when they daub the landscape with streaks of gold and patches of pale yellow, and then cast their leaves upon the first autumn gales with a huge prodigality, like Timon of Athens giving away his fortune.

And elms in winter, raftering the sky on some crisp day when you walk beneath them and look up through last year's rooks'-nest at 'the cold and rook-delighting heaven.'

I love the elm at all seasons of the year. I even love it on a winter night when we put the big logs on our fire.

People say elm is 'a sulky burner,' and so it is when it is wet. 'Elm-wood burns like churchyard mould' runs the rhyme.

But when the logs are dry, and have lain two or three years since cutting, they burn slowly and steadily, giving out a great heat; a big log will glow for hours like a furnace at the centre of the fire.

To painters...

No tree contributes more to the character and the familiar pattern of pastoral England; no tree has meant more to our great landscape painters, such as Constable and Gainsborough.

But today we are losing our precious elms at a greater rate than any other trees – partly through the deadly elm-disease (a fungus which gradually rots them), partly though the widening of roads, which causes the loss of much hedgerow timber, and partly through the sheer insensibility and selfishness of many farmers, whose dislike of hedgerow timber is only less than their loathing of isolated trees.

Their shade

Both 'waste' a little ground – and are worth a few quid when they're down though they're 'worth nowt when they're standing.'

In fact, it is true that the shade of elms is less inhibiting to the growth of grass than that of most other trees.

Elm is therefore the perfect tree for giving summer shelter to beasts at pasture. Nowadays many farmers deny that such shade is necessary.

'The cows gives just as much milk without it.'

No woods

The old-fashioned farmer cared more for the comfort of his cattle. It must be miserable to stand out among the flies in a shade-less field on a hot day.

How content by comparison the beasts look as they stand in the cool grass underneath some huge elm, that was planted maybe in the days of Queen Anne.

There are several kinds of elm to be found in our English hedges. The Wych Elm (or Wych Hazel) sometimes grows to 120 feet, with a girth of 50 feet or more

It propagates itself mainly by seed whereas the English elm, which is straighter and more slender, though often as tall, spreads itself by sucker.

It has always puzzled me why you never see a wood of elms; spinneys, yes, and little coppices, but the elm is as rare in woodland as it is common in hedgerows.

Another thing about the elm which always surprises me is its family relationship; it's a cousin, believe it or not, of the stinging nettle – and the rough hairs along the midrib of the leaf possess to a smaller extent the same irritant quality as the nettles have.

Tough

In the old days elm was in great demand by wagon builders, wheelwrights and shipwrights – its timber made tough tackle-block after pickling in salt water mud.

Longer ago still – in ancient Rome – elm-rods were used for the punishment of slaves; another grim association for the tree which loves not man.

It's still used for coffins, wherever in the world the elm-tree grows;

Elm hateth
Man, and waiteth.

Why the Colonel hated Cats

When your sitting-room carpet suddenly sprouts a small mound or hummock and this mound or hummock proceeds to move quite quickly from one end of the room to the other, you may be forgiven for thinking you are seeing things that aren't there.

However, I turned up the end of the carpet and rolled it back, revealing as soon as it reached the little mound none other than a mole trying frantically to scratch his way down through the floorboards.

No need, when any creature appears unexpectedly in *our* house, to ask how it got there.

The cats! It is endearing but sometimes embarrassing that they should wish to show us everything they catch.

One of them had a blitz against the rats which from time to time trouble us, and for a whole week laid a rat a day neatly upon the doormat.

The rats were dead; but sometimes the hunters' trophies are very much alive.

I have known an eel-fisher cat who was apt to leave slimy eels a foot long wriggling on its owner's hearth!

And there are plenty of cats which are dab-hands at snake-catching – if you possess one you may sit down and find a grass-snake beside you on the sofa.

Such trophies as a rule are liberated unharmed. So was our mole; both cats and dogs find moles distasteful.

Shrews are likewise unpalatable, so when one of the cats brings in a shrew it drops it quickly and the terrified thing runs round squeaking until somebody picks it up and takes it into the garden.

Sharp nip

Whoever does this kindness generally gets bitten for his pains; a sharp little nip, said to be toxic, but harmless in my own experience.

Moles can nip too, but are more likely to scratch, and they have powerful forelegs which they work with a side-ways, oar-like motion – as if they were Blues winning a boat-race.

The mole I fetched out from under the carpet was very angry indeed; it both scratched and bit.

I carried it outside, couldn't decide what to do with it, was somehow affected by its own sense of urgency, and dropped it over a low wall among the lettuces and the rows of peas.

The Colonel

Then I said to myself; surely I must be the only ass in the world who would deliberately let loose a mole in his vegetable garden.

You can't stop a cat hunting; it's the nature of the beast.

And though I'd certainly rescue a robin from the very jaws of death, mice are a different matter, and in their case I do not believe it's any of man's business to intervene between predator and prey.

I know the game seems cruel, and the temptation to save the small and helpless victim from the large tormentor makes a strong appeal to our chivalry.

The old Colonel I have often written of in this column, who spent all his days when he wasn't drinking whisky in hunting, shooting, fishing, badger-digging and setting ingenious traps for stoats, weasels and rats – this ferocious old fellow was so trigger-happy that scarcely a bird save robin and jenny wren was safe when he prowled round his fields.

Himself...

Nevertheless he had a grievance against cats because 'the beggars don't kill to eat they get a sort of beastly fun out of it.'

There couldn't have been a more precise description of his own activities, but the dear old chap was incapable of seeing this.

So if ever he observed a cat playing with a bird or a mouse he would rush to the rescue of the bird or mouse with all the high-mindedness of a Knight of the Round Table saving a maid from a dragon.

The paradox was complicated further by the fact that he himself was a great enemy of mice.

And towards the end of his days when he was drinking an awful lot of whisky, so that the frontiers of reality and fantasy became a trifle blurred, he suffered from a minor persecution mania concerning mice, genuine or imagined.

Nipped!

He set traps by the score, and was always getting his arthritic old fingers hurt by the Little Nipper going off at the wrong moment. (I put a little bit of him, this aspect at any rate, into the character of Perdo in my last novel 'The Waters Under the Earth').

But if the Colonel saw a cat tormenting a mouse it was a very different matter.

'Get off with you, you savage cruel brute! Get out of my sight! And let the poor little beggar go.

'You're twenty times as big as he is. Let me have him or I'll... Poor little beggar!

'Frightened was you? Has the damned great brute hurt you at all?'

He became so concerned about the menace of mice, as he conceived it, that in addition to the Nipper he laid all manner of traps for them.

The Flowers' last Spring

'Ripeness is all.' The three wild ducks which all laid enormous clutches of eggs in the tops of our old willow-trees are hatching off their brood s and tipping them out of the tree-tops.

They fill the stream with little balls of fluff which dart to and fro as fast as those beetles called water-boatmen, which skate on the surface of the water.

A bantam hen clucks over her chickens. The senior cat, Toffytoes, purrs with pride as she suckles her latest kittens. Her daughter Panda is obviously going to have kittens soon.

My mare Zena (of whom you are bound to hear a good deal more in the next few weeks!) is in foal to the son of a Derby Winner and due on May 15.

The only frustrated ones at Lower Mill Farm are the little Siamese, too young to be mated, who is howling the house down like 'woman waiting for her demon lover.' and I myself, still undelivered of the novel I've been working at for more than a year, and which I do not expect to finish for another three or four months.

My springs

If only I'd got my novel done I should take more time off this season. Each year as I grow older and my prospective springs get fewer I say to myself with Housman:

And since to look at things in bloom
(So many) springs are little room
About the woodlands I will go
To see the cherry hung with snow.

And to see also, what is to me the quintessence of this season, the young green coming on the beeches with the dappled sunlight slanting through upon the sheets of bluebells underneath!

It's queer how the colour of the bluebells changes the farther you get away from them.

Standing there between the beeches, you see a lake of clear blue; but if you look at the bluebells from afar – say on the slope of a hill across a little valley – the shade is cobalt.

And if you see them from the air, as I have often done, flying a Moth 300 feet above the Cotswold hills, then all the brightness seems to have drained from the bluebells and the patches look slate-grey with only a tinge of blue; the colour of a cock-chaffinch's topknot about this time of year!

Alas!

Although our wild bluebells are hyacinths, the fat flowers in our gardens derive from an exotic, eastern species, *Hyacinthus orientalis*.

Why 'Hyacinthus'? He was a Greek youth whom Apollo loved and killed by accident when he was throwing the discus.

From his blood sprang a flower of which the petals were marked with the letters *ai* – 'Alas!' in Greek.

I have read that some foreign member of the Lily tribe really does bear on its petals such markings; but our English bluebell doesn't and was therefore named by the old botanist Linnaeus, *Hyacinthus non-scriptus* – 'not written on.'

Reservoir

At this season of flowers let us spare a thought for some very small and unspectacular ones which have been growing undisturbed in a part of Upper Teesdale for the past 10,000 years, but will shortly disappear for ever when 70 acres of the valley are inundated to make a new reservoir.

This is needed to provide a stop-gap water supply for the increasing population of the north-east and to quench the gargantuan thirst for industry in those parts.

Some botanical communities unique in the whole world will be destroyed when the dam is built and the water rises up behind it.

Botanists of many nations fought hard against the proposal, and the Bill to authorise it was contested tooth and nail in the Commons and in the Lords.

But eventually utilitarianism won as it was bound to do; since it's difficult to set the value of a few rare little flowers – even though they happen to be the sole surviving remnant of an Ice Age flora – against a big new factory.

I daresay some grave, elderly and distinguished scientists in places as far apart as Sweden, Switzerland and the United States, wept salt tears when they heard that the fight was lost in England's House of Lords, and that the small flowers, which matter so much to so few people, were to be sacrificed in favour of the reservoir, which matters to so many.

I shrug...

For my part, I shrug my shoulders in sadness, for I know that the urgent needs and the quenchless greeds of mankind will always win when they come into conflict with such trivialities (as they seem to most people) as learning and beauty.

Shakespeare gave the same sad shrug four and half centuries ago when he wrote:

> How with this rage shall beauty hold a plea,
> Whose action is no stronger than a flower?

Kisses Behind the Stuffed Whale

A tree-trunk at Caversham, near Reading, used to bear a notice-board nailed to it, with the following stern warning:

CAUTION TO BUTTERFLY CATCHERS
Any One found Disfiguring the trees, for the purpose of taking Moths, will be Prosecuted according to Law. Any Person giving information of the Trespass will be rewarded by
J. D. Blount.Esq.

The trouble was that the 'butterfly catchers' liked to go 'sugaring' for moths.

At dusk they painted streaks of black treacle boiled up with sugar and flavoured with rum upon the trees lining a bridle-path.

Later they did the rounds with killing-bottle and lamp, catching the moths with had been attracted by the aroma.

A campaign

The sticky patches on the trees offended the landowner, who conducted a long campaign against the bug-hunters.

They included (in the 1880's) a professor or two, an official of the Hope Museum at Oxford, and – believe it or not – a *lady* bug-hunter who was apt to steal a march on her rivals by sending her coachman to 'sugar' all the most desirable trees in the afternoon, so that she could lay claim to them later.

Her competitors then had a long walk to the far end of the bridle-path, until they could find some unclaimed trees on which to paint their treacle.

Can't you imagine those grave late-Victorian bug-hunters, bearded or dun-dreary whiskered, wearing Norfolk breeches and deer-stalker hats, sleuthing along the bridle-path like shaggy versions of Sherlock Holmes! Pockets bulging with glass-topped pillboxes in one hand the killing-bottle, in the other a 'bullseye lantern'?

The minions of J. D. Blount Esquire would be able to sniff 'em afar off, because of the museum-smell of naphthalene pervading their clothes.

Museum-smell

That fusty, musty, napthaleny museum-smell, shall I ever forget it? I was a dedicated and devoted naturalist by the time I was ten.

That year or the next I was taken to London for the very first time by a kind but fussy aunt. She offered to show me Westminster Abbey, the Houses of Parliament, the Tower of London.

Oh, bother all that, said I; all I want to see is the Natural History Museum at South Kensington. And there I spent the whole of my two days in London.

From ten o'clock in the morning till five o'clock at night I walked in awe and delight among the stuffed things and the skeletons, pored over the cabinets of birds-eggs and the drawers full of butterflies...

And my aunt, who dared not leave me for long in case I should escape from her charge in the huge and dangerous city, spent most of the two days in the Museum also. She told me later that she never wanted to smell naphthalene or look into a pair of glass eyes again.

Museums in those days were very solemn places. The hush was rather like the hush inside a cathedral; the elderly grey round-shouldered keepers and their assistants seemed to go on tiptoe among the exhibits, the way old vergers walk when they show you round the ambulatory...

In some towns the museum was the only public building (apart from the churches) open on Sunday. In Wales and Scotland even the pubs were shut on a:

> *Dreary, drizzly*
> *Granny's own grizzly*
> *Dismal Municipal Sunday,*

as A. P. Herbert described it in a poem. He pictured the young couples going to the museum in search of warmth, shelter and privacy, and being chivvied by the attendants when they tried to steal a kiss, hidden behind the stuffed whale.

Gladly pay

Things are happier for them nowadays! According to Mr. Francis Cheetham, the kindly Curator of the Norwich Castle Museum, the courting couples gladly pay their entrance fee for the purpose of 'necking' in the dimly-lit bird room.

'It is one of our jobs to provide a public service', says this most humane of museum-men, according to a report in a newspaper.

'The young couples are some of our best-behaved visitors. They have no time for vandalism.

'We often find that after a time they actually become interested in the exhibits.'

Maybe; though if I were a young man I don't think I would exchange the look in my girl's eyes for the cold gaze of the eagles, the steady stare of the owls.

The reward

But, Mr. Cheetham goes on, 'I think the couples pick the bird-room because it is just like being in the countryside, but in the dry. They marry, and then bring their children along to see the birds...'

So maybe science will reap the reward of its toleration in a new generation of ornithologists – Peter Scotts and James Fishers as yet unborn!

Here's Pomposity – it takes the Bun

A note upon my desk says that 'The Rodent Control Officer will call...'

As usual, it makes me furious. I shall be only too pleased to see the ratcatcher, who is a decent fellow; but Rodent Control Officer – I ask you! The best ratcatcher I ever knew was a very distinguished biologist who was given the job of organising a campaign against rats and mice during the war, when our dwindling food-stores held against emergency, were threatened by a massive infestation of pests.

He carried out his experiments in the field, personally, crawling about sewerage plants in filthy old clothes, rats' tails sticking out of his pockets, and in his haversack a selection of deadly poisons by comparison with which the apothecary's shop at Verona was as harmless as a village grocer's. He described himself at that time, with pardonable pride as 'the only Old Etonian ratcatcher.' But not a Rodent Control Officer, heavens no!

❖　　❖　　❖

I suppose that small officials in small posts like to call themselves officers because it makes them feel important. But they forget that it also makes them into a music hall joke; Rodent Control Officers are now fair game for every variety artist. As time goes by and they become still more pompous they will probably form themselves into a Rodent Control Officers' Association and appoint a public relations officer to make protests about jokes made about Rodent Control Officers.

This is by no means so extravagant an idea as you may think. Not long ago I wrote a feature programme about Dartmoor for the B.B.C.; I had a party of coach-tourists in it, and wrote a part for a facetious Cockney guide. I subsequently received a solemn official admonishment from the Guild of Guide Lecturers (a body of whose existence I was previously unaware), reproving me for making the guide funny. I respectfully wrote back that 'Punch' and the 'New Yorker' would soon be out of business if associations representing dentists, doctors, policemen, farmers, sergeant-majors and what not were given the right to censor all the jokes about dentists, doctors, policemen, farmers, sergeant-majors, and so on.

※　　※　　※

I did read somewhere, as a matter of fact, that some organisation representing the police had made its protest to the B.B.C. against 'the uneducated way in which policemen were made to talk on the wireless.' Bless their hearts, they wanted Oxford accents! About the time when I heard of this protest I met a much funnier policeman than I'd ever heard on the wireless. I was the witness of an accident, and I went to the police station to make a statement. All went well until I said 'I was going towards Worcester,' when I noticed that the constable had written down 'I was proceeding towards Worcester.'

'Look here,' I said, 'you write down what I say. After all, I've been trying to learn the right way to use words for 25 years or so; it's my trade, and I ought to know a bit about it.'

'Proceeding is correct,' said he. 'You've got to say proceeding.'

'Then I shall refuse to sign the statement.'

He sighed.

'Very well, sir. But 'going' isn't right. It ought to be 'proceeding,' really it ought.'

※　　※　　※

First prize for pomposity goes, however, not to the police, nor the Guild of Guide Lecturers, who must on no account be made fun of, nor even to the Rodent Control Officers, but to a milk trade protection society whose Argus-eyed secretary saw a film called 'Father Brown' in which Alec Guinness, in a very funny scene, shied a few milk bottles about.

The secretary thereupon wrote to the film company concerned gravely requesting them to cut out the offending scene. 'We are considerably alarmed at the possible repercussions that can well result if this particular scene is exhibited throughout the United Kingdom.' Everybody, I suppose, would be liable to emulate Alec Guinness and start breaking milk bottles!

❋   ❋   ❋

That takes the bun. And mention of the bun reminds me of G. K. Chesterton's poem against grocers:

God made the wicked Grocer
For a mystery and a sign
That men might shun the awful shop
And go to inns to dine.
He crams with cans of poisoned meat
The subjects of the King,
And when they die in thousands,
Why, he laughs like anything.

It only remains for the grocers' trade organisation to demand that those verses be immediately expunged from the 'Oxford Dictionary of Quotations.'

❋   ❋   ❋

And now I must see my ratcatcher. *Hamelin's town in Brunswick, By famous Hanover city,* I seem to remember, once suffered from a plague of rats. I must ask him whether the Pied Piper was a past president of the Rodent Control Officers' Association.

The Ducks in my Dictionary

For me the greatest time-waster, but also the most delightful, is the big 'Oxford English Dictionary.' in 12 volumes. This morning in an old book I came across a word with which I wasn't familiar.

The word was 'ducible' which obviously meant 'easily led'; but it seemed a rare one, so I looked it up in the O.E.D. Next to 'ducible' my eye caught the word 'duck'.

Now ducks at the moment are very much in my mind – our wild ducks are nesting and in the stream outside my study window all the ornamental waterfowl are making love; so I thought I'd satisfy a moment of curiosity concerning the origin of the word 'duck'.

Surprisingly the O.E.D. didn't know for sure, though in a couple of learned paragraphs it suggested that the name was related to old words in various languages meaning 'do dive'.

Cure-all

But, being the O.E.D., it led me on. There are various definitions of duck.

One of them is 'the flesh of this fowl'; and Goldsmith is quoted: 'Plutarch assures us that Cato kept his whole family in health by feeding them with duck whenever they were out of order.'

Fascinating; duck as a cure-all. By snippets such as these the O.E.D., whenever I open it, persuades me to do no work at all for the next half hour.

'Phrases and Proverbial Sayings' came next; I read a quotation from 'The Water Babies':

Then he turned up his eyes like a duck in thunder.

Do your ducks do so? I must watch them next thunderstorm.

Then comes another definition: 'A term of endearment.' Shakespeare, it turns out, was the first to call a girl 'Duck' – in 'A Midsummer Night's Dream'.

Then we come to 'Anglo-Indian Slang': 'Duck' was a nickname for 'Soldiers of the Bombay Presidency.'

'Bombay Duck,' however, is quite a different kettle of fish. It is a fish, dried in the sun and 'always served with a curry'. (Very beastly it is too. The infallible O.E.D. mentions its 'peculiar flavour').

Half-way

Ten minutes wasted, and I was only half way through the words connected with 'duck'.

A 'lame duck' on the Stock Exchange is a chap who cannot meet his financial engagements. So there are Ducks as well as Bulls and Bears.

The cricketer's duck – my duck, I say to myself, for the whole of my cricketing career has been played to the tune of a quacking of ducks – is short for duck's egg because its shape is like a nought.

But why duck's egg? Why not hen's egg, which is much more the shape of a nought – or pigeon's egg or owl's egg, which are perfectly round?

Should not my usual Saturday afternoon score be more appropriately described as a Hen or a Pigeon or an Owl?

A duck's wife, I read, is 'a woman who has charge of ducks.' This is an admirable description of my wife at this time of year.

I will call her a duck-wife and see what happens… Duck-oil is an expression for water… Duckweed grows in ponds… The Duck-billed Platypus is known as Duckmole in Tasmania…

And so on and so on. 'A duck' can mean an 'instantaneous lowering of head or body, a rapid jerky bow'. How apt – for I look out of my study window and see our drakes performing this very obeisance to their ladies!

But 'duck' can also mean a quick plunge or dip. 'The older women content themselves with a few ducks as the waves break over them (1876).'

At once the sentence conjures up a picture of those extraordinary bathing machines, those remarkable bathing costumes that did not expose one square inch of flesh – compare them with bikinis today!

Throwing

While I mentally compare them with bikinis, the minutes tick away.

I tear myself from such thoughts, and turn to 'Duck and drake' – 'A pastime consisting in throwing a flat stone or the like over the surface of water so as to cause it to rebound or skip as many times as possible before sinking.'

Could you have defined it better or more tersely? I bet you couldn't.

When did the pastime get its name? The O.E.D. goes back to 1583, and shows that the game was then played with oyster shells; and believe it or not, this marvellous compendium of language gives 14 more dated quotations to illustrate the use of the phrase 'Ducks and drakes.'

And so we go on. Did you know duck-hawk was a name for the marsh harrier? Duck-egg is a colour... Ducks-bill is an instrument used in surgery... Ducklingship is the state of being a duckling – how limitless is this English language of ours!

The moral (since we have now apparently reached a point where we need one) is don't open the Oxford English Dictionary when you are supposed to be writing your County Column for the week!

This Nonsense about Home-made Wine

In this cold spring, most seeds have been slow to germinate; but none slower than the parsley, which 'you always look for long before it shows.'

They have an old saying about it in our local. 'Before it comes up, parsley goes to the devil and back three times.'

There are lots of country saws and old obscure jokes about this homely herb. For instance – 'The missus wears the breeches where parsley grows well.'

In my part of the Midlands it's often made into home-made wine; but rather surreptitiously, because of an extraordinary superstition, that parsley wine is an aphrodisiac.

Nobody is very ready to boast that he is brewing a sort of love-potion for himself or for anybody else!

So you don't hear a great deal from the wine-makers about their marvellous vintages of parsley wine. But they make it all the same!

Beastly

Concerning other home-made wine, we have, year in, year out, a running argument in the local.

The people who make this stuff (out of dandelion, parsnip, nettle, elderberry, damson, sugar-beet, raisins, marigolds, and Lord knows what) are given to inordinate boasting about its exquisite flavour and unbelievable potency.

Regarding the flavour, they can boast as much as they please. I think it's almost always beastly – though I've had a gooseberry wine and a cowslip wine which were certainly drinkable.

But this is a matter of taste, about which you can argue for ever. What is not arguable is the fact that whatever you put in it, and however long you keep it, you cannot by fermentation alone make a home-made wine that is stronger than, let us say, a claret or burgundy or any other 'bought' wine you care to name.

It doesn't make a ha'porth of difference how much sugar or yeast you add to the vegetable brew; it doesn't matter whether you use mangold-wurzels or elder flowers (which make a wine that tastes like hair-oil) or ripe Victoria plums or rhubarb or for that matter lawn-mowings! Whatever you do, the maximum strength of your home-made wine will be round about 15 degrees of alcohol.

If you can drink a bottle of claret without getting drunk, you can likewise drink a bottle of anybody's dandelion or damson wine without getting drunk, unless, of course, the wine-maker has cheated by adding brandy, rum or whisky to the mixture.

Farm Cart

Belief

I don't say the home-made wine won't hurt you. The particular esters of alcohol produced by wine fermented under uncontrolled conditions may, for all I know, give you a worse headache than those you find in decent claret.

But I do firmly maintain that all these stories about the fearful potency of home-made wines are simply old wives' tales.

I have heard men telling each other in awe-stricken whispers that they possess a bottle of grandmama's parsnip wine or grandfather's rhubarb, '*fifty years old come Michaelmas*,' and they really believe that the older it is the stronger it is.

This is sheer nonsense of course; when fermentation is finished in a matter of months nothing can make the wine stronger save the surreptitious addition of a tumblerful of spirits.

Then, if the victim has previously been to the pub and drunk half-a-dozen pints of beer, a glass or two of home-made wine might have some of the remarkable effects which the old men attribute to it.

Real good

"'That's real good,' George says to I, after he'd took a thimbleful of my old mother's mangel-wurzel. 'I could do with another little 'un,' 'e says to I. 'You better be careful,' I says to 'ee, and I pours out no more'n another thimbleful into 'is glass.

"'Here's to your old mother,' he says to I – bless her, she's bin in her grave more'n a score of years. Then, he say suddenlike, 'It be waarm in 'ere, beant it?' he says, and then as if 'e'd bin poleaxed, down he went plonk in front of the fireplace, you ought to a-sin 'im, arter just two thimblefuls, lying there as if 'e was jud…"

My Hat

It possessed the greenish dignity of age. It was the sort of hat which is the envy of all men and the bane of all men's wives. Women alone saw no beauty in it; that greasy band, which it wore as naturally and as honourably as a patriarch wears his grey hairs, was an offence and abomination in their eyes; and they hated its weathered crown because it was shapeless and soft.

Twice or thrice they even did violence to it, as a vandal might knock an arm off the Discobolus or wantonly shatter the taut bowstring of Eros; I recovered it from the dustbin, bought it back dearly at a jumble-sale, and snatched it off the head of a beggar to whom it had been given in lieu of alms. It suffered so many vicissitudes, was saved so often from horrible dooms, that I began to think it was immortal.

And now it is gone forever.

※　　※　　※

So when I arrive in England I must buy another hat; I must wear upon my head some stiff, strange thing that has not known the wind and the rain; I must endure the hateful congratulations of women, who will admire my purchase because it is new and shapely and horribly clean. Soulless as they are, how shall they know that it has no virtue in it because it has not been with me, like that other one, in the grey mountains of Wales and Scotland, has not fished with me and shot with me and stalked with me and climbed with me, has not known the great wind of Glyder Fawr nor the cold mists of the Cairngorms, nor the sweet rain of the Sierra Nevada?

Alas, it was there, in Andalusia, but three weeks ago, that my old hat achieved its greatest triumph, became suddenly memorable and historic, a national possession rather than a personal one. I had landed but ten minutes previously, and was feeling slightly lost and shy, as I always do when I first set foot in a foreign land. I paused in the street to light a cigarette and was suddenly accosted by an elegantly dressed person who rose from a seat outside an inn and addressed me in English.

'Good day.'

'Good day,' I said, surprised.

'I spik ze Engleeesh very well, yes?' said the elegant person.

'I'm sure you do.' I agreed.

'You haf ze Engleesh cigarettes – very good,' he remarked. He extracted one from my open case. I smiled tolerantly.

'I haf with me a friend,' he said, and extracted another.

Tudor House,
Tewkesbury about 1920

Then he shook me warmly by the hand and returned to his seat. I began to feel a fool, and hurriedly crossed the street; but before I did so I heard his friend say to him in Spanish, as he returned with his booty;

'Well done! How did you manage it?'

'Oh it was easy!' he replied. 'Only an Englishman would wear such a hat!'

After that I was more proud of it than ever; it had become, as it were, a symbol of my British origin; I felt that even if I lost my passport my old hat would take me safely home. It told silently of brown dripping coverts, and hacking down country lanes, and guns and fishing-rods, and all English country things.

And now, ah, now the cold waters have it, and the green swaying weeds; deep-sea fishes goggle at it with big eyes; horrible luminous creatures are probably nesting in it; or Davy Jones himself wears it upon his head.

I was leaning over the rail, watching Finisterre fade into a faint loom behind us, when a gust of wind came suddenly and carried my hat twenty yards before it fell. Now it is vanished, and sad waves are sighing over it and I hasten to write this tribute before it is forgotten.

Perhaps, after all, this fate is the best that could have happened to it. At least – I comfort myself – there are no scarecrows in the sea.

Country Causerie

One rarely sees a good scarecrow in the country nowadays; for that matter one rarely sees a scarecrow at all, for the modern substitute is a contrivance which produces a loud bang every 10 minutes or so. The pigeons seem to get used to the bang, however; at most it causes a brief flutter, after which they return to their pastime of pulling off the shoots of the young peas.

To tell the truth, they never took very much notice of the old-fashioned scarecrow either. Enormous ingenuity was spent on some of these objects. Grandfather's old top hat was perched at a rakish angle on the turnip-head, the old frock coat was stuffed out with straw, black trousers were stiffened with stout stakes planted firmly in the ground.

I don't know why the scarecrow was always over dressed for the country, nor why it nearly always represented a man, hardly ever a woman, since surely the farmer's wife would be more likely to possess cast-off clothes, and more willing to hand them over.

The only female scarecrow I can remember was dressed from top to toe in the fashion of the 1920s; cloche hat, short skirt, waist-below-the-hips. No wonder the farmer's wife had been glad to give that outfit away; and it stood in the cornfield for many weeks as a memorial to the most hideous fashion, surely, ever invented by man and worn by woman. Every time I saw it I was shocked afresh by recollection that such a costume had enshrined all romance for me at the age of 18.

Yes, I had fallen in and out of love with those stove-pipe creatures peeping out so coyly from under the horrible cloche hats. Mr Michael Arlen, whom we read avidly in those days, had written a whole novel, *The Green Hat*, romanticising such a head-dress.

Taste changes as often as the wind, and ever and anon it returns to the same quarter. Who reads *The Green Hat* nowadays? Who can remember its brittle style, self-conscious as the laughter of those

Bright Young Things whom it glorified and its 'daring' plot which would have shocked our mothers if they had understood what it was about?

Shades of Tallulah Bankhead, shades of thc Charleston, shades of the 'bob' and the 'shingle' and the 'bingle'... If I mock that scarecrow, I mock my own youth.

Had it both ways

From scarecrows to witches (not a far cry after all); the other day upon the 6-inch ordnance map I discovered a curious field-name. *Witchpond Wold*; and when I explored the place, lo, there was still a pond there, and a very nasty one, deep, muddy, covered with scum, and overhung by melancholy willow. I daresay they did duck 'witches' there or perhaps it was worse than ducking, for there was at one time a convenient theory about witches; that if they sank they were innocent, and if they floated they were guilty; so the mob had it both ways.

The very thought of those 17th century witch-hunts makes one sick with horror.

We are always astonished afresh at the superstitious barbarism of our forebears. But we'd better not be too cock-a-hoop about our own condition of unsuperstitious civilisation. Some noble and justified words by Lord Samuel last year, commenting upon the state of our morals, was the signal for such a yapping and howling among lesser men, in the Press and elsewhere, that we very nearly had a completely hysterical witch-hunt on our hands, in 20th century Britain!

And America, where they once burned a lot of 'witches' and where in quite recent times they have lynched a lot of negroes in circumstances just as revolting, is at present indulging in a witch-hunt on a remarkable scale. I am told that if you were seen 20 years ago having a drink with a mildly left-wing intellectual you are liable today to be suspected of Communism. The superstition of our ignorant forebears hardly went farther that that.

Crazed Beldams

That there were crazed old beldams who believed themselves to be witches I do not doubt, nor that there were foolish and timid people who died because they imagined a 'spell' had been put upon them.

A good and wise man, John Selden, writing a little after Shakespeare's death, put the whole matter of witches in a nutshell when he declared; 'The law against Witches does not prove there be any, but it punishes the Malice of those People, that use a such means to take away Men's Lives. If one should profess that by turning his Hat thrice, and crying Buz, he could take away a Man's Life, though in truth he could do no such thing, yet this were a just Law made by the State, that whosoever should turn his Hat thrice, and cry Buz, with an *intention* to take way a Man's Life, shall be put to death.'

Let's Stop Killing
the Things we Love

'Each man kills the thing he loves,' wrote Oscar Wilde in Reading Gaol. The line comes into my mind whenever I read of some new well-meaning proposal for 'improving the access' to our last lonely wild places, arguments for the provision of car-parks so that more people can enjoy the remote countryside, and so on.

I think it is utterly wrong to do so. The mountains and the moors remain wild only because it is at present difficult for large numbers of people to get to them.

If we make it easy, by providing proper roads instead of footpaths, we shall kill the thing stone dead.

For goodness sake, let us leave the enjoyment of these last, remote fortresses to those few who want to visit them so much that they are prepared to put up with some minor discomforts; e.g. a 20-mile walk over rough tracks, perhaps a lonely night on a mountainside.

Disturbance

Certainly it will be impossible to conserve some of our wilder plants, birds and animals if the wild places which they inhabit are 'opened up' in the way that is being suggested.

I do not so much fear that the birds will be persecuted and the flowers torn up – though this will certainly happen – as the general disturbance of the environment which inevitably happens where you get large numbers of people parking cars, playing games, picnicking and so on.

Inevitably, there is a gradually increasing demand for 'facilities' of various kinds. So many people run out of petrol that planning permission is given for one discreet petrol station.

If there's a petrol station, why not let it sell pop and ice-creams – for which there is naturally a growing demand.

Bottles and cartons mean litter. Litter means litterbins. They are doubtless as well-designed and as discreet as the so-called conveniences for which there will certainly be a demand.

Too late

Suddenly – too late – we become aware that half-way up the mountain we have planted a little bit of suburbia. It will grow and grow.

Should there be some very rare plant growing handy, the Botanical Society or somebody will probably have to urge the National Trust, or the Nature Conservancy to put a fence round it.

On the fence will be a very neat discreet notice board with the plant's name done in the same well-mannered lettering as the word LITTER on the bins:

LADY ORCHID
Orchis Purpurea

and scores of hundreds of people will be able to lean over the fence and gaze at the Lady Orchid blooming in its season.

But nobody any longer will have the exquisite delight of finding the rare flower for themselves.

So with the birds and the beasts. I do not know of any rare wild thing that loves a crowd of humans.

Indeed, most of these creatures are rare because they cannot adapt themselves to living in close association with mankind and his works.

(Conversely, rats and mice and sparrows and starlings are common because of their association with man).

Therefore, the more we 'open up' the wild places, the more artificial becomes the condition in which the surviving wild creatures can be seen.

The nesting kite has to be guarded night and day and watched only from a special hide provided by courtesy of the Royal Society for the Protection of Birds.

How long before even the red deer have to be fenced into enclosures and looked after by keepers?

Yet we started off with the best intentions in the world. We said: Here is a beautiful moorland, but it is largely wasted because it belongs to Lord X and is only enjoyed by Lord X and his house-parties in the months of August and September when they come to shoot grouse and stalk deer.

How long?

So by a mixture of persuasion and legislation we gained access for the public to use paths through the moor. We put up a youth hostel there. We scheduled the whole district as an Area of Outstanding Beauty and part of a national park.

So far so good.

But how long before it becomes a sort of cross between a Whipsnade and Hampstead Heath?

Then with its litter-bins and notice-boards, with its self-conscious 'conservation' of animal and flower, it will no longer be lonely or wild (which were precisely the qualities which led us first to take an interest in it).

It won't even be an Area of Outstanding Beauty any more: for
Each man kills the thing he loves
By each let this be heard...

Why I said 'Accidia go to Blazes'

I often think that naturalists are among the luckiest people in the world. For no journey can ever be a bore to them and every change of scene offers them something new, interesting, even exciting, to watch and study.

The other day, for instance, my wife and I thought we needed a little holiday; just four days in the Brecon Hills. It rained most of the time; that scarcely mattered. The flowers were quite different from the flowers at home, because the soil was acid, whereas ours is calcareous.

As I walked over the empty wet moorland, my feet brushed through acres of bilberry. It's ages since I saw bilberry in flower, because I usually go to the moorlands in the summer or autumn, when it's in berry.

Again, it was a ferny country; and ours is almost bereft of ferns – apart from the bracken, which is an agricultural nuisance, but looks charming at this season of the year, when its curled-up fronds are unfolding like the paws of a sleepy kitten.

Lower Mill Farm

In Wales, however, there were ferns everywhere, enough to make me realise how little I knew about them.

Sprigs

After all, there are less than fifty different sorts in Britain; a man who calls himself a bit of an amateur naturalist ought to be able to recognise most of them

I can't; so I brought home some sprigs of the doubtful ones and compared them with the excellent coloured illustrations in a Victorian textbook called 'The Ferns of Great Britain and their Allies' by Anne Pratt.

If there has been a comprehensive book on British ferns published since then, I confess I do not know of it.

Miss Pratt's charming volume was originally published – and printed much better than most books are today – by the Society for Promoting Christian Knowledge.

One of the greatest naturalists that ever lived – T. H. Huxley – was an agnostic and invented the word to describe his condition of 'not knowing'.

As for pantheism, I have always had a lot of sympathy for the Greek who thanked Poseidon for the wonder of the sea, Artemis for the joy of the chase, Aphrodite for love's mysteries; and for the Roman who paused at the wayside shrine to thank Faunus for the woods and their beasts, and Flora for the flowers.

For my part, though I have never been able to believe in a personal God, I can discover intimations of divinity in every manifestation of nature's beauty, wonder, and complexity; in a bacillus seen through a high powered microscope just as much as in a sunset or a primrose; in the otter and the fox; in a galloping horse or a leaping salmon; or indeed the unfolding frond of a fern.

It seems to me quite proper, therefore, that the Society for Promoting Christian Knowledge should have thought it worth while to promote the knowledge of such exquisite things as ferns.

The birds in Brecon were different from ours – though we'd driven less than a hundred miles from home.

Before I'd walked a hundred yards up the swift little Irfon river I'd seen two dippers with smart white shirt fronts disporting themselves on the rocks.

I'd watched a yellow wagtail trying to teach two of her fledglings to do a first solo from a rock on the bank to one which stood up like a jagged black tooth parting the white waters only a dozen feet away.

Nuthatch

I saw a nuthatch, and a tree-creeper scurrying up an alder-trunk like a little brown mouse; and another bird which we never meet with in my part of England, though it's common enough in Wales.

When I first set eyes on it beside a mountain stream I thought it looked like a tiny, toy magpie; it was a pied flycatcher.

Its cousin, the spotted flycatcher, comes every spring to my garden, and generally nests there.

But the pied flycatcher is rare save in the west and north, and is specially a bird of central Wales.

To a Welsh naturalist this little black-and-white bird, tweeting its quaint little song which has been likened to 'Tree, tree; Once more I come to thee'- would have seemed so commonplace that he'd have scarcely noticed it.

But to me it gave as much pleasure as the pair of buzzards circling high over the hills. Which brings me back to where I started; wherever a naturalist goes he finds wonder and delight; and so the worst of the Seven Deadly Sins, Accidia or boredom, passes him by.

For my part I've committed most of the others, and enjoyed some of them very much, but as long as I have eyes to see and ears to hear I shall continue to say to old Accidia 'Go to Blazes!'

The Elizabeths share
a Love of Horses

In 'Elizabeth and Leicester', that excellent history by Elizabeth Jenkins, I read of a bill sent to Lord Robert Dudley, Master of the Queen's Horse, by a veterinary Quack of those days. "For Bay Bell, founded in the fore-feet 'so much'."

'For Bay Star, dressed under the belly'... 'For dressing of the carriage mule's sore foot'... 'For dressing Grey Jennet on the shoulder'... 'For dressing Bay Prince of his sore eye'... 'A drink for the pled colt' 'A drink to Jenny Ringrave,' 'A drink to Bay Altabelle.' 'For dressing of Bay Minion'... and so on.

Fascinating

The names of the horses are fascinating. Some are called after members of the Court – Hastings, Hunadon, Arundel, Killigrew.

Others are pleasantly fanciful, Bellaface, Gentle, Gray Sparrow, Speedwell.

The Queen, it seems, was as fond of horses as is her Royal namesake today.

Lord Robert, in 1560 or so, was writing to Lord Sussex in Ireland begging for some horses to be sent over 'for the Queen's own saddle, especially strong, good gallopers, which are better than her geldings, which she spareth not to try as fast as they can go.'

❈　　❈　　❈

The vet's accounts catalogue many of the curiously-named diseases to which horses are subject... 'the *Farcy*,' 'the *Stranglion*' and such-like.

But Shakespeare, in 'The Taming of the Shrew', has a still more wonderful list of them.

The meanings

Blondello is describing the horse on which Pegtruchio came to his wedding:

> 'Possessed with the glanders, and like to mose
> in the chine, troubled with the lampas,
> infected with the fashions, full of wind-galls
> sped with spavins, rayed with the yellows,
> past cue of the fives, stark spoiled with the
> staggers, begnawn with the bots, swayed in
> the back, and shoulder-shotten...'

Just for fun, I looked up some of these dreadful disorders in the Oxford English Dictionary.

The *fashions* turns out to be another version of the *farcy* or *glanders* – boils inside the nose.

The *lampas* is a swelling inside the horse's mouth. The *yellows* (I might have guessed) is jaundice.

The *fives*, which puzzled me most of all, turns out be a corruption of 'Avives', an old name for the strangles, which you might call a sort of horse-mumps, a swelling of the parotid gland.

❖   ❖   ❖

What's more, the fives apparently affected humans as well! For I find (in Dame Edith Sitwell's 'English Eccentrics') an account of a 16th century quack offering to cure 'the most common Body of Man, the names of which are as follows: *The Strong Fives, the Marhambles, the Moon-Pall and the Hockogrockle.*'

A woman quack, according to Dame Edith, was offering remedies about the same time for such feminine disorder as 'the *Glimm'ning of the Gizzard,* the *Quavering of the Kidneys.* and the *Wambling Trot.*'

No explanations

Even the well-nigh infallible dictionary fails me over some of these. To wamble, it tells me, is to suffer from nausea, to feel sick.

For the rest, it forbears to speculate concerning the *moon-pall*, which sounds to me like a love-sickness of the very young.

It does not mention the *marthambles*; and, alas, it has never heard of the *hockogrockle* either, that 'most common Distemper incident to the Body of Man.'

Broadway Tower,
Worcestershire

Sea Hero's Pocketful of Acorns

It is a pleasant little compliment that his people paid to King Charles II when they wore the sprigs of oak in their caps on May 29 – his birthday and the day he came home again after his exile.

But oak-apple day isn't, of course, the anniversary of his hiding in the Boscobel Oak: that happened after his defeat at the Battle of Worcester in September 1651.

I read somewhere that visitors to Boscobel used to collect acorns from the tree, to plant them in his memory, and that some enterprising spiv used even to sell genuine Boscobel acorns at a penny apiece!

People would plant them in their gardens so that their grandsons could point proudly to 'an oak sprung from an acorn of King Charles' oak.'

❂   ❂   ❂

I approve of people who plant acorns. Admiral Collingwood, that great and good man, had a little country estate which he loved more than he loved seafaring, and it is said that whenever he was home he would walk about his fields with a pocketful of acorns, popping one into the ground here and there.

He was planting acorns just before Trafalgar! Then he went off to the battle and it was he who observed when the glorious signal fluttered out from the Victory: 'I wish the Admiral would not make so many signals. We all know what we have to do.'

Earlier that day, having shaved carefully, he put on silk stockings because 'if one should get shot in the leg they would be much more manageable for the surgeon,' and thus dressed for the occasion he addressed his officers: 'Now, gentlemen, let us do something today which the world may talk of hereafter.'

He certainly knew what he had to do. He set every sail in the Royal Sovereign and raced the Victory into battle. 'See how that

Memorial Cross,
Tewkesbury

noble fellow takes his ship into action,' said Nelson. And Collingwood engaged by five of the enemy simultaneously, grinned: 'What would not Nelson give to be here.'

He was wounded (in the foot so the silk stockings came in handy!) but he was much too modest to mention this in his despatches, which he wrote in splendid prose which matched the triumph and the tragedy of the day. His letter to the Admiralty 'moves with the dignity of an anthem.'

❈   ❈   ❈

He never saw his oak-saplings growing. He longed to return to his estate after Trafalgar, but the politicians were nervous. Nelson was dead, and Collingwood was the next in stature of the great blue-water sailors.

England wouldn't feel safe unless Collingwood were at sea! So for four and a half years, eating his heart out, he sailed the Mediterranean, searching the seas which Nelson had swept clear of foes for an enemy that would never dare to challenge him.

How he longed for home! 'Then will I plant my cabbages and prune my gooseberries,' he wrote, 'cultivate corn and twist the woodbine through the hawthorn hedge with as much satisfaction in my improvement as ever Diocletian had, and with the same desire and hope that the occasion may never occur again to call me back to more important but less pleasurable duties.'

But it was not to be. He died at sea, in 1810, and they carried him home and laid him beside Nelson, to whom he had been as a brother.

❈   ❈   ❈

I don't know if any of his oak-trees grew up to maturity; if so they should now be in their prime.

What better memorial to one who was at once so brave and so gentle, so steadfast of purpose, so stout-hearted that he regarded a shower of shot as much as a shower of snowflakes.

Tyrant in the House

Six months ago we bought a little Siamese tom, with sealskin ears and speedwell-blue eyes (except in certain lights, when they burn a dull geranium-red). His long hind legs gave him a sort of seaman's roll as he waddled round the house, inspecting it; and he as he did so he muttered softly to himself in a strange un-feline tongue.

There was an air of such truculence about him that we called him Hodge, a truculent-sounding name which was borne originally by the most remarkable cat in history, the household pet of the great Dr. Johnson.

Little is known about this fabulous animal except that the mighty man of letters treated it with an indulgence which amounted almost to subservience. For instance, when Hodge grew old and sick he refused to eat anything but oysters; and Dr. Johnson would drag himself daily to the fish market on his poor dropsical legs to buy oysters for the fastidious brute.

He could have sent his negro servant on the errand, but with fine sensibility he decided that "Francis' dignity might be hurt, at seeing himself employed for the convenience of a quadruped." In spite of all our levelling-down and our boasted democracy I wonder if we possess such a sense of human dignity to-day.

❋ ❋ ❋

The tyranny which Hodge exercised over his master was not confined to sending him on errands. Dr. Johnson, it seems, dared scarcely to speak his mind in the cat's company. Boswell, who hated cats and 'suffered a good deal from the presence of the same Hodge' visited Dr. Johnson one day in his rooms. Hodge was scrambling on the great man's breast apparently with much satisfaction, while "my friend, smiling and half-whistling, rubbed down his back and pulled him by the tail; and when I observed he was a fine cat, saying

'Why, yes, sir, but I have had cats whom I liked better than this,' – and then, as if perceiving Hodge to be out of countenance, adding: 'But he is a very fine cat, and a very fine cat indeed.'"

On another occasion, describing the despicable state into which a young gentleman of good family had fallen, Dr. Johnson observed: "Sir, when I heard of him last, he was running about town, shooting cats." "And then," says Boswell, "in a sort of kindly reverie he bethought himself of his own favourite cat, and said, 'But Hodge shan't be shot; no, no. Hodge shall not be shot.'"

❀   ❀   ❀

It is quite clear that what really happened on these occasions (though Boswell, a cat-hater, failed to notice it) was that Hodge gave Dr. Johnson a Look. If you understand cats, you recognise that Look. It is a gentle reminder of who is the real boss and although Dr. Johnson in his famous dictionary was not over kind to the cat, defining it as 'a domestic animal that catches mice, commonly reckoned by naturalists the lowest order of the entire species,' there is no doubt who was the master in Dr. Johnson's household.

Hodge, in fact, could quell with a glance this tyrant of the coffee-houses, who in the course of half an hour's talk 'tossed and gored several persons,' as Boswell put it. In a moment the cat's cold and luminous eyes could reduce him to silence; and that is a feat which no human being ever achieved. Hodge must indeed have been a formidable animal.

❀   ❀   ❀

And now I perceive – or imagine I perceive – the same characteristics appearing in his namesake, our little Siamese tom. This new Hodge has fought his way, and sometimes merely glared his way, to the top of the feline hierarchy in our household. He has deposed, one by one, the other cats from their favourite chairs and their favourite hunting grounds; and now he is starting on us.

When he addresses us, it is simply to inform us that he requires some food to be provided or some service to be performed. He doesn't mew; he says '*Way-ow-oo*' in a tone of muffled thunder; and I can almost fancy in that tone an echo of Dr. Johnson himself expressing some forcible opinion. Like the doctor, he is dogmatic to the point of being rude; there is no arguing with his '*Way-ow-oo*'. These fish-bits are not very fresh: buy me a piece of whale-meat; *Way-ow-oo!*

He has just taken to roving o'nights, a practice which his mistress disapproves of, holding that he is too young for such adventures. The order was given that he was to be kept in. But last night at half past ten he strode to the front door and muttered. I hesitated, and he gave me a Look. Still I hesitated, and the thunder rumbled deep down in his throat. '*Way-ow-ow!*' And I fancied suddenly that I could hear the very accents of Dr. Johnson laying down the law: "Sir, whoever thinks of going to bed before twelve o'clock is a scoundrel!

Meekly I opened the door.

Farm Plough

Not Everyone Likes Buttercups

Everybody agrees that it's been a great year for buttercups. I haven't seen the meadows so golden since I was a small boy.

Then a walk across Tewkesbury Ham at buttercup time would gild my bare knees with a layer of pollen so thick they stayed yellow until I washed it off.

However, not everybody likes buttercups. Cows find them acrid, I think, and I'm sure it isn't true, as I used to be told, that the rich colour of farm butter in June is due to the cows eating plenty of buttercups at that time.

Never again

That's another memory which takes me back to my boyhood; the butter was always 'farm butter,' much yellower than 'shop' butter, and of quite a different consistency.

When you cut it, minute beads of water were squeezed out by the knife and glistened on the cut surface.

I daresay I shall never again taste butter as good as that farmhouse butter which I used to plaster on the crusty corners of cottage loaves when I came back ravenous from fishing or birds nesting in holidays long, long ago.

But, as I was saying, cows don't like buttercups; nor do modern farmers – I heard two deploring them on the radio the other day.

'I hate the things myself,' said one. The other seemed to equate the proliferation of buttercups with the decline of good husbandry, by which he really meant efficient spraying.

The fact of the matter is that the majority of farmers nowadays hate to see any flower growing anywhere in their fields; they feel it must be robbing them of something.

I wonder...

But I wonder whether buttercups in meadows, as distinct from pasture fields, really do much harm?

In the years between the wars, when I was learning to be a country auctioneer, I learned a good deal about hay, which was always involved in our farm valuations.

Now there was no weed-spraying in those days; and we made some of our best hay in the riverside meadows where the buttercups grew so thick that you could scarcely see the grass.

Yet I swear that in good seasons both the yield and the quality were as good as that of any hay we make today.

The acrid taste of buttercups probably disappears when they are withered.

At any rate the cows did well and so did the great Suffolk Punch ploughing-horses do well in the buttercup hay that was made in the lush meadow beside the Avon by old-fashioned farmers who bore no malice against flowers.

Big straw hats were always the rig for haymaking. Face, necks and arms were burned brick-red by the sun.

The men and women were out in the fields from soon after dawn until it was nearly dusk.

You had to start early, because it was too hot for the horses to work at mid-day.

You therefore started cutting as early as possible – two horses pulling the mowing machine – and you rested from noon until mid-afternoon, lying under a hedge, munching your 'bait,' drinking pints of cider which you'd sweat out of you in no time when you started work again.

Tired horses with their noses in bags of wetted chaff flicked their tails at the flies which hummed, hummed all about them, so that the whole drowsy noontide seemed to be filled with a gentle buzzing.

Among the swathes grasshoppers chirruped.

From the middle patch still unmown came the rusty-rasping *kek-kek* of the corncrake – a sound which we in the midland counties will probably never hear again, since the once-common bird has become quite extinct here.

Meadow brown butterflies, graylings, ringlets, all the cigar-coloured grass-loving butterflies of high summer danced their mazy dances round the edge of the field where the old bone-rattling tedding machine was pulled by some pensioned-off old favourite, brought back from the paddock to help with the haymaking.

Shepherd's hut

Like a horse in a dream, old Dobbin plodded along; a girl in a bright-blue dress, brown-face Meg the farmer's daughter, drove the tedder and flapped the reins on Dobbin's back when he looked as if he was falling asleep.

The hay kicked up by the turning tines of the tedding-machine seemed to spurt up behind it like a ceaseless brown fountain.

Behind the machine came two more girls raking the hay into rows with wooden rakes.

But my eyes were mostly on Meg's blue dress, I remember...

Heigh-ho. That was more years ago than I care to reckon. And now it is a different world, in which farmers hate buttercups and soon the butterflies will dance no more.

Before I am done with buttercups, let me record that I found a large and splendid one the other day; the Globe Flower, which I'd never before seen growing wild in Britain.

I was walking up the valley of the Irfon, in mid-Wales, and in a damp pasture near the river I spotted some yellow flowers which were much bigger than ordinary buttercups and yet much paler than marsh marigolds.

Even from 50 yards, they were unmistakable; Trollius Europaeus, whose lemon-coloured sepals are curved inwards so that the big handsome flower becomes a globe, a little Chinese lantern glowing in the sun.

It's a rare joy as you get older to find a wild flower you've never seen before.

I hope the beautiful Trollius survives, among the orchids and ladysmocks and kingcups which made that Welsh field as flowery as our English fields were long ago.

I can just imagine what those two farmers whom I heard talking on the radio would have had to say; 'Disgraceful. Ought to be sprayed.'

Urban Tidiness that is Killing Nature

During the war, when it often seemed to me that My Lords of the Admiralty, whenever they had an idle moment, must have said to themselves; 'Where's that chap John Moore? Let's send him somewhere else.' I certainly got a chance to have a good look at the British Empire before the sun set on it.

I learned that one of the small, touching idiosyncrasies of Englishmen abroad was their passion for lawns.

Wherever I went in desert or jungle, parched or flooded, half-frozen or tropical places, there was always a lawn.

Small bank officials in Caribbean islands, small traders in West Africa, all sweated on Sundays to mow, weed, trim and neatly cut the edges of a patch of grass, which declared on their behalf, defiance of the proliferous jungle and homesickness for some such places as Surbiton or Sutton Coldfield – where there were even better lawns.

Ubiquity

Blitzed Malta, rocky Gibraltar, used precious water to sprinkle lawns which made bits of them look a bit like England.

In late Canadian springs, snow melted to reveal unexpected lawns, that grew green quicker than you'd think possible and had to be mown twice a week in late May.

Landing upon odd little airstrips in a Swordfish or an old bumbling Walrus, taking my captain or admiral to pay his respects at Government House I would always find a marvellous official lawn from which every daisy, plantain or more menacing tropical weed had been removed by naval or army defaulters.

I watched those defaulters all over the world, crawling upon their knees with little trowels or forks called widgers, getting rid of the weeds, so that the grass at G.H. might match the grass at, say, Roehampton, where they play croquet.

Nostalgia

This care and cherishing of lawns went on even at the darkest hours of the war, when London was getting its nightly blitz, and therefore a patch of mown grass; two or three thousand miles from London evoked an almost unbearable nostalgia.

It stood, I suppose, for peace and all the sweetness and silliness of peace, shirt-sleeved suburbanites pushing mowers at week-ends, tea on the lawn (wasps and all), striped umbrellas clock golf, deck chairs with Sunday papers lying beside them that had no crises headlines, but were chockfull of delicious murders which seemed hugely important in those days before tens of thousands of people were being killed every day.

So I confess I have wept salt tears at the sight of a lawn, especially when there was a flagpole upon it, and the Union flag coming down at sunset, long shadows and a bugler.

But today, more than 20 years later in an ever-more-suburbanized England, I begin to have my doubts.

Lawns multiply wherever the housing estates creep out; and upon each petty patch, every week-end some smug though sweaty fellow, contemplating his daisyless, plantainless rod, rood, or perch, seems to say to himself in triumph; 'I'm the boss. Nature's finished here. *I've* fixed her.'

Terrifying

Tidiness terrifies me. It is not so much the pesticides or the weedkillers which threaten the utter destruction of all wild life in England, but the passion for suburban tidiness, as typified by a lawn.

Upon outskirts of towns, or round the edges of villages where new houses have been built, you can see how tidiness-for-its-own sake destroys not only the character of the whole area but the last hope for survival of the wild things which still live there.

For suburban man is not content with his lawn. If there's a grass verge in front of his house he has to make *that* too into a strip of lawn.

Why?

He sweats away, clipping and mowing it – why? To prevent a few wild flowers growing there!

Opposite him, maybe, there's another grass verge. White umbels grow up in it haphazard every spring – with many other plants some to be described as 'weeds.'

Suburban man can't tolerate that, so he invites the council to spray the opposite verge with hormone weedkillers, grass-growth inhibitors and what not, so that nature can no linger exist *opposite* his little green garden gate.

Flowers? He'll tell you he loves flowers; and so he does, so long as they remain his subjects, good citizens of his tiny domain, subservient, controllable.

Old Cottage at Bredon

Depressing

That's why suburban gardens depress me. They're so unlike the old cottage gardens, where the flowers grew as if they were enjoying themselves, hollyhocks, stocks gillies, pansies, not too orderly, no little Hitler running the show.

If butterflies fluttered round those flowers it was because a few weeds were allowed to grow along the outside edges of the garden, breeding-places for insects, feeding-places for seed-eating birds and nectar-loving bees.

Co-existence

Thus in the villages man contrived to live with nature, and the happy co-existence of gardeners, birds and insects was assured.

The ex-townsman or suburbanite, buying or renting a house in the country today, doesn't want to co-exist. He must be the boss, all the time, all over his little kingdom.

If a clump of weeds appears anywhere, even a growth of rough-grass along his boundary fence, he dabs away at it with a paraquat spray so that it withers and goes brown.

He strangely prefers a withered herb to a green one; a close-cropped verge to a flowery one; for his worship is tidiness.

Wild nature and tidiness do not go together. Tidiness wins.

Why the Sparrows can have my Flowers

A market gardener made an interesting comment in our local the other day.

He said "them clever chaps that mixes up p'isons 'as gin us sprays to beat the weeds and all sorts of concoctions to kill the creepy-crawlies; but nobody can tell me how to save my crops from the perishin' birds."

It is perfectly true that here and there in the Vale of Evesham the birds are making certain sorts of market-gardening impossible.

Pigeons are an uncontrollable pest; in hard winters they take a heavy toll of the sprouts and in summer they are a plague among the peas.

I know two or three men who have given up growing peas because of the damage done by pigeons in the late stages and by sparrows when the first shoots appear.

Already this year in my small vegetable garden hordes of sparrows have ripped to pieces four rows of winter lettuce.

It'll heart up in the end and the crop won't be lost, but it will be two or three weeks later than it would have been but for the attentions of the sparrows.

If I were a market-gardener growing lettuce on a big scale, those two or three weeks might make all the difference between a fair profit and a heavy loss – for winter lettuce has a short season and the price is always good at the beginning, bad towards the end.

I put in three plum-trees a few years back. Though they should be in full bearing now, I haven't had a plum off them; bullfinches regularly tear off the buds.

I used to grow polyanthus in my flower beds in the spring. The sparrows would always tear off the first yellow petals but they spared the other colours, and the flowers generally made a good show in the end.

Nowadays it's quite useless for me to grow polyanthus. The sparrows go for all colour impartially and tear to bits every flower until the plants are exhausted and will bear no more.

'Batfowlers'

Are there more birds? There are certainly more bullfinches; and I think there are more sparrows.

In the old days bullfinches may have been controlled to some extent by birdsnesting boys, and sparrows were certainly controlled by the 'batfowlers'.

These boys used to beat them out of ivy on winter nights, catch them in strawberry netting held between long poles and roast them

Abbey Mill,
Tewkesbury 1940's

on spits over the fire when they were so delicious they were called 'poor man's pheasant.'

The boys not only had the fun of sparrow-catching by torchlight and their feast to finish off with, but were often paid a bob or two by the owner of the ivy-clad wall, who remembered what the sparrows might do to his peas in the spring.

Killing off

Nowadays we seem to be at once foolishly sentimental about common birds and wickedly destructive of the rare ones.

We are killing off our owls, hawks and falcons – even the great golden eagles of Scotland – by the pesticides which we use against insects. (The insects are eaten by small birds and the poison lives on in their tissues, so that it is later ingested by the predators who feed on them).

Despite the terrific impact of such books as Rachel Carson's 'Silent Spring' we do very little to limit the use of these pesticides.

Yet when a country pub cooks a sparrow pie for its customers – an event which got into the news recently – there's a general outcry about the wickedness and cruelty of killing the poor sparrows; though nobody complains about people eating game pie, rabbit pie, or for that matter pork pie!

Indeed, our attitude to nature is so mixed-up that I often think we want our heads looking at; we are capable of being both soppy and destructive like kids.

Ruthless

However, I'm glad our attitude to the sparrows is not quite so ruthless as that of the young Chinese.

A few years go the regime let it be known that since sparrows stole the People's Corn their existence could no longer be tolerated.

In every township and village hordes of youths chivvied and killed every sparrow that chirped; and not only sparrows, for all birds were sparrows to them.

They practically wiped out every small bird within range of the centres of population; and since many were beneficial ones I daresay caterpillars by the million ravaged the People's Cabbages.

Emptiness

A fiend of mine who visited China not long ago was at first bewildered, then horrified by the lack of bird-song, the emptiness (as it seemed to him) of a world where no feathered thing was permitted to perch or to fly.

Later he noticed another manifestation of the People's revolting utilitarianism; there were no domestic pets.

He asked what had happened to the dogs and the cats; and he was told that they wasted food which belonged to the People, so had been put down.

In Peking, believe it or not, he saw only one Pekingese; and that belonged to the British Embassy.

An Embassy official took it for a walk on a lead every day; and the Chinese would turn their heads almost as if it were a rarity, observing it with curiosity or perhaps contempt.

So after all, I'm glad we don't unduly persecute our bullfinches or conduct large-scale warfare against sparrows.

The former can have my plums, the latter my polyanthus.

Better that than the horrors of utilitarianism, the mean and miserable outlook which regards all creatures that on earth do dwell simply in the light of their usefulness or otherwise to Man.

So I unwished those Beavers

I have been putting a couple of dams in my little stream (curiously known as the Squitterbrook) in order to make two small pools where I can grow waterside plants and waterlilies.

Damming a stream isn't as easy as it sounds.

Unless you design your dam very skilfully the whole thing silts up, so that you create a mudbath instead of a pond or perhaps instead you create a large area of marsh through water seeping through the shoulders of the dam.

Water is devilish cunning in all sorts of ways. It waits until you've planted your waterside plants then mysteriously and unbeknownst to you, erodes the bank underneath them.

The bank, with your precious plants, then falls into the water and helps to silt up your little pool.

Helpers

In all this trickery the mischievous water is aided (in my stream anyway) by the water-rats, which dig their holes under the banks, helping along the process of erosion, or – worse still – make miniature mine-shafts which enable the water to by-pass my dam altogether.

I love water-rats but at the moment they are driving me crazy.

Now if only I had a family of their second-cousins-twice-removed, the beavers, they'd build my dam for me; and it would really work, because beavers are much better at water engineering than I am.

In Canada they use their sharp incisor teeth as saws, to fell willows, aspens, birches and poplars.

They cut them into suitable lengths, push them into position, then add mud and stones, so that the dam 'by frequent repairing becomes a solid bank, capable of resisting a great force of both ice and water; and as the willow, poplar and birch generally take root and shoot up, they by degrees form a kind of regular planted hedge.'

Authority

So says Mr Hearne, an authority on Canadian beavers.

The industrious rodents build houses, their 'lodges', out of the same materials as they use for the dams.

'They carry the mud and stones in their forepaws and the timber between their teeth. They work at night and with great expedition.'

Beavers are about 3ft long, nosetip to tailtip. About four grown-ups, and six or eight youngsters, inhabit each family-sized 'house' which they build for their winter quarters.

Were there, once upon a time, beavers damming the Squitter-brook, which I so ineffectually try to dam?

There may have been. The European beaver, which is a close relation of the Canadian sort, is still found in the Elbe, Rhone and Danube, and in parts of Scandinavia.

Trusting

There were still plenty of beavers in Britain when William the Conqueror was King.

But they became extinct during the following century – it is thought about 1150 – presumably because beaver-fur was so warm and sought after, and because the tame and trusting animals were easy to trap or to shoot with arrows.

I have read that one of the last habitats of the beaver in Britain was the River Telfi, in Wales.

Upon that lovely tumbling river, at a place called Pontrhyd-fendigaid, near strangely-named Yspitty Yspeth, some Cistercian monks built an abbey 600 feet up in the hills.

It was called Ystrad Fflur, which is surely a Welsh version of the Latin *srata Florida*. In Latin 'strata' means a straight paved way; florida is 'flowery.'

So we get a charming picture of the situation of this abbey high up on the Telfi.

But it's cold in winter, up in those hills and if, as we're told, there were beavers at Ystrad Fflur, the monks no doubt killed them and cured the skins to make themselves warm hoods and gaskins.

But as it happened the beavers outlasted the monks, at the abbey built beside the flowery way.

For some reason the shaven men departed, and the building was allowed to fall into ruin, early in the tenth century. The beavers remained there for another 200 years.

Breakfast

Working (like a beaver!) to repair my amateurish dam, and damning the water-rats that have made it leak again, I wished there were still some beavers in Britain today.

That was until I went to my reference-books and read their life-histories and learned that 'their favourite food are the water-lilies, Nuphar and Nymphaea, which grows at the bottom of lakes and rivers.'

Nuphar and Nymphaea are the beautiful plants for whose benefit I made my dams in the first place; so I promptly unwished the beavers, for my two cherished waterlilies, which cost me 30s apiece, are sending their first tender leaves up towards the surface of the water.

They would just about make a breakfast for a beaver if one came swimming up the Squitterbrook this morning...

Nature's Colour Charts

Each season, in our Midland countryside, has its own colour-motif, its special series of matching and contrasting shades. The very early spring is predominantly yellow – celandines, buxom marsh-marigolds, primroses, and hey the doxy over the dale! Gradually the yellow is replaced by white, submerged rather in a foaming flood of whiteness of which the hedge-parsley at the lanesides is the lovely spume and spray.

The month of May comes forth, like the maids in Thomas Hardy's poem, 'Sprig muslin drest,' and then almost imperceptibly this new-laundered whiteness curdles upon the landscape exactly like milk creaming in the dairy pans. By hawthorn-time it is all curds, and then comes the first meadowsweet, creamy again, and the hemlock-kind standing up in the damp places.

※　※　※

Just now, at the end of June, there is another huge scene-shifting of the seasons, and the stage is set with the dark reds, the mauves, the reddish-purples which somehow match the sultry dog-days. It's heather and heath on the peaty hillsides, wherever there is an acid soil; but on the limestone, where heather cannot grow, the rose-bay willow-herb is a splendid substitute, one shade redder, perhaps, but painting the hillsides with just as broad a brush.

On the river banks, meanwhile, Nature writes her Purple Patches with loosestrife – a name, by the way, which is supposed to be a corruption of love's strife, though I don't know why the conflict and turmoil of love should be associated with this particular colour.

It strikes me that the cottage garden flower, Love-Lies-Bleeding, is the same shade; wounded hearts must be the notion behind it. My old gardener used to write on the wooden labels where he planted this flower; *Lovelies Bleeding*. Goodness how sad!

✺   ✺   ✺

They make a long catalogue, the red-purple flowers of July. There's ragged robin and red campion; there are wild vetches and fields of cultivated lucerne; and here and there, though locally, cranesbill soaks a whole meadow with its sanguine stain. Then there are those sullen dark flowers of the dog-days, comfrey and horehound and the deadly nightshade itself; hanging their heads, shade-loving, reminiscent somehow of the prose style of Edgar Allen Poe, all thick curtains and velvet upholstery and each of them as wickedly sultry-looking as Miss Lauren Bacall's publicity agent would like us to think her to be.

Indeed, almost all the flowers of late summer seem somehow to match the thundery mood. Spring flowers possess a daintiness, an innocence, the freshness and delicacy of maids; those of late autumn blaze with a defiant and devil-may-care glory, sort of 'We who are about to die salute thee' air.

But the flowers of midsummer, they belong to the shadows; they are sisters of the fenny snake and the toad, innocence is a stranger to them, they have no freshness, and they flaunt themselves, as a rule, in the dank untrodden places, where in olden time the tall herbage knew only the tread of white witch or black who for good or ill crept out at moon's eclipse to gather them.

✺   ✺   ✺

I had forgotten the foxgloves, of all July's flowers the most showy and splendid. I know some woodland rides – in the Forest of Dean particularly – where at this season the foxgloves are like an army with banners, companies, battalions, brigades on the march; you can walk for miles and never reach the rearguard of that column. And somewhere in almost every red spike there is sure to be a pollen-smudged bee burrowing into a flower, buzzing merrily as she follows the line of purple dots towards the sweet centre.

It was unaccountably delightful, when one was a child, to pluck a flower or two and draw them over one's small grubby nails, cool fingerstalls; and we were told then that they were folk's gloves really, gloves for the fairies, foxgloves being a mere slurring of the ancient name. It may be so; but it sounds to me suspiciously like the invention of a Victorian nursery-governess.

Foxes live where foxgloves grow, anyhow; of all flowers Digitalis is the fox's flower, standing about his earth, sheltering him from his enemies. But foxes or fairies, who cares? The Chinese, I learn from a book I have just been reading, believe in fox-fairies, 'weird and beautiful creatures', haunters of graveyards yet regarded as friendly spirits, delighting, not affrighting those lucky enough to encounter them.

A fox unhunted, is lovely indeed; but a fox-fairy – I can imagine few things lovelier!

Brown trout

Mullet, Sense and Censorship

I'm just back from what was meant to be a fishing holiday in Ireland; but I was frustrated by a recently-broken arm and my fishing was limited to the contemplation of an enormous shoal of grey mullet, which inhabited an inlet of Bantry Bay, at the bottom of my host's garden. My good fellow-contributor, Mr. Thurlow-Craig, may be able to tell me how to catch grey mullet; I fancy he could catch anything. But the Irish hold it to be an impossibility.

Mr. O'Leary, collecting seaweed for manure, told me he had often tried to encompass them with a Seine-net. "'Tis no use at arl! No sooner is the net beneath them than they'll be leppin' into the elements!" Likewise Mr. O'Shea at the tackle-shop roared with laughter at my idea of catching them on a rod.

"Whoever heerd of sich a notion now! 'Tis impossible arltgether."

"But they must eat *something*," I said. "They must take some bait."

"A very onclane fish is the grey mullet," said O'Shea the Fishing Tackle.

"But what do they feed on?"

"Feelth!"

※　　※　　※

Nevertheless "grey mullet" appeared unashamedly on the menu at the little hotel in the so-called Town (population 950). So I asked the landlord by what baited hooks, nets or engines of mystery they had been caught. The answer was surprising.

"No mystery at arl! We shoot them."

"*Shoot?*"

"Pepper the shoals with a shot-gun."

Was the Englishman having his leg pulled? I wondered. But the landlord seemed as serious as it is possible for an Irishman to be; which is never very serious.

"Och now, if you order them for dinner you'll see the shot-holes in them and you'll be after spitting out the lead-pellets onto your plate!"

I did not stay to dinner, however, so I have no proof that when it's close-season for snipe the Irish go mullet-shooting. Over to Mr. Thurlow-Craig!

※　　※　　※

Quite a brief stay in Southern Ireland serves to rid one of the popular English idea that the Irish are a casual and inefficient race. Too often, I am afraid, we have been apt to describe as "charming but hopelessly inefficient" the peoples we have ruled; and then have discovered with bewilderment (and too late!) that they were capable of "making things work" without us.

The processes of Government, communications and services work very well in Eire, and the average peasant cultivates the poor land with skill and industry. I couldn't help wondering what some of our Evesham market-gardeners would say if, before they planted a crop of potatoes, they had to make about 20 three-mile journeys down to a beach in a donkey-cart to load, and carry up a steep hill, the sea-weed which is the only available organic manure!

And if, before they could light a fire on their hearth in the winter, they had to make as many journeys up a 1000-foot mountain to the bog to cut, dry and carry the peat, which is the only available fuel!

Yet these peasants, who work and live so much harder than us in our fatter land, are the gayest and the merriest poor men I have ever met.

※　　※　　※

Another thing one notices in Eire is that they build well and they build quickly; their new houses (of all sizes) are nicely designed and fit into the landscape better than many of ours because, wherever possible, they build in stone or use colour-wash, which is always preferable, I think, to unweathered and staring brick. I cannot understand why we do not colour-wash more of our new council houses – in the countryside at any rate; for oddly enough a whitewashed or pink-washed house seems to fit into any landscape – as one sees in Ireland, France, or Spain.

They build, these Irish, but they do not repair. Everywhere are abandoned ruined cottages which perhaps were too far gone to make habitable; and there are still the blackened ruins of the Big Houses too, a grim reminder of a time which, perhaps, both we and the Irish would be wise to forget.

How strange, I thought, that people who fought with such terrible and bitter passion for their freedom should deliberately saddle themselves with a censorship, of books and magazines which is the very negation of freedom! The fact that the Irish censorship banned my own last novel is of no importance either to me or to the very few Irishmen who otherwise might have read it; that intelligent Irishmen should not be allowed to read the works of their own George Bernard Shaw (*Saint Joan,* for instance) or of Sean O'Casey seems to me to be shocking indeed.

It is their own business, perhaps; certainly my Irish friend will hasten to make it plain to me that it is none of mine; yet censorship is a totalitarian and evil thing wherever it is found and I see no reason why one should hesitate to speak one's mind about it – in a country where it is our priceless privilege to speak our mind about anything under the sun.

Taking the Cat for a Walk

As a naturalist I like to walk alone. Human companions chatter; and even the best of dogs get over-excited and go argy-bargying about, frightening the wild creatures which I want to study. But now and then I take a cat for company.

This Dick Whittington habit surprises people who think of cats in terms of firesides and laps. But I have always found that a favourite cat, whether Siamese or ordinary, is easily trained to go for cross-country walks. It is better company than a dog; for it stalks in the same way as I do; it follows the advice which Izaak Walton gave to anglers: Study to be Quiet.

A naturalist can learn a lot from watching the way a cat goes about its hunting.

The best huntress we ever had was called Candy. In the autumn when fat voles were plentiful, she would sometimes take me hunting along the lee side of a hedge. She went a few yards ahead of me, glancing round now and then to make sure I was there. She walked delicately, lifting her paws high between steps.

Retriever

Then suddenly she would stop dead, listen, twitch ears and nostrils; a tiny ripple would run along her tail just before she pounced. Killing the vole outright she would bring it to me as if she were a retriever, and lay it at my feet accompanied by the tuft of grass which her strong jaws had closed on as she seized it.

When I had picked it up she immediately resumed her hunting; as if she employed me to carry her game! I once found myself holding four fat voles by their tails, while Candy farther along the hedge was hunting a fifth. I saw myself in my mind's eye, embarrassingly ludicrous dangling Candy's two brace as I dutifully walked behind her.

Sentimental

On such occasions when she seemed to be out for a record bag she never bothered to play with her victims before killing them. This 'cruel' game is distressing to sensitive people, whose chivalry is aroused by it.

I knew an ardent foxhunter who became so enraged by the spectacle that he rescued the mouse and drove off the cat! But surely this is sheer sentimentality.

Every moment of every day, in the fields and woods and hedges, doubtless in your garden too, goes on the ceaseless savagery of predator to prey. I don't believe it's any part of man's business to impose his moral law on nature, so I allow the cat to play with her mouse in the way her ancestors learned to do (doubtless for good biological reasons) long before man with his morals appeared upon the scene.

For what biological reasons? Kitten training is an obvious one. I notice that our cats always start their kittens on very small mice; often on pygmy shrews, though these are never eaten, and probably have an unpleasant taste. If pygmy shrews aren't available, the cat hunts for half-grown field-mice.

Playmates

The size of the victim is perfectly matched to the capabilities of the kittens. As they grow older they are given bigger mice to play with.

An odd and rather disturbing aspect of the play is that sometimes a kind of sinister affection seems to come into it. The cat cuddles the mouse as if it were one of her own kittens.

A cat belonging to a friend of mine brought a field-mouse into the house alive and for some reason 'adopted' it. Predator and prey lived together in amity, and drank milk from the same saucer. And once a cat of ours called Duffy caught a vole on our frozen stream where it was nibbling some crumbs which had blown off the bird table, Duffy played with that vole all day, sliding on the ice as he chased it. The vole seemed to be playing too. Once it ran up to Duffy as he lay on his side, and cuddled up to his warm and furry belly. Duffy never killed it; though there was a nasty moment when he held it between his front paws and began to wash its head. At last he put its head into his mouth and pretended he was about to devour it!

Unaccountably he opened his mouth wide and let the vole go. Then he yawned; and the vole, crouching beside him in quivering astonishment watched with small black shiny eyes. At last it scurried away across the ice; and Duffy, tired out by the game or perhaps simply bored, stretched out a long foreleg as if in farewell, slowly opening and closing his claws.

Field gate,
Lower Lode Lane

Plum Jerkum

In Gloucestershire, as is well known, we are great ones for home-made wine. Before the war – when sugar was plentiful – no cottager lacked his little store, and the *Dandelion 1920* or the *Plum Jerkum 1921* were regarded in much the same light as a rich man looks upon his precious vintages, the great years of claret and burgundy and port.

Very often the wine was kept for ten years or even longer; it was saved up for a silver wedding or a son's coming-of-age. I once drank some raisin wine which was 25 years old; it tasted like syrup of figs, and was very nasty.

The flavour, however, or perhaps I should say the bouquet, is not the most important thing about home-made wine. Plum wine often tastes of prussic acid, which I think it actually contains, having absorbed it from the plum stones. Elderflower wine tastes of hair oil. Potato wine tastes of the earth and of things long dead. No matter. We are concerned not so much with the taste as with the potency. The ambition, in fact, of my very provident people is to achieve the maximum effect with the minimum bulk. They aim at producing a wine of which one small glass is enough to make a strong man's head go round. Moreover, they sometimes succeed; and when this happens old ladies who consider themselves to be teetotallers get much innocent enjoyment out of drinking it in thimblefuls.

Now there is naturally a good deal of argument about which raw materials make the most powerful brew. It is generally agreed that the choice lies between mangold wurzel and sugar-beet, and thereafter the pundits differ. Last winter the matter was put to the test in a rather curious way; but the test was inconclusive. You shall hear the story, and you shall judge.

Frankie Jones, our local horse-dealer, was minded to buy 'a little cob suitable for a lady' from a rival dealer some five miles away. He first fortified himself with some of his own mangold wine, of which he is very proud, and set off by bus. For some reason the bus was late, or he missed the earlier one – at any rate he didn't arrive at his rival's establishment until the late afternoon. This wouldn't have mattered if he had bought the cob as he would then have driven it home. Unfortunately the animal failed to please him. He had it trotted up and down in the yard, shrugged his shoulders, and offered ten pounds for it with the air of one giving a large sum to charity. His rival said; 'You're joking, old chap,' and roared with laughter; the price, he added, was thirty-five pounds. At this Mr. Jones likewise roared with laughter, and you would have thought the hard-bitten pair to be the jolliest fellows in the world.

They haggled for a bit in a half-hearted way, and got very cold; so Mr. Jones's rival invited him in to have a glass of sugar-beet wine. They continued to haggle while they sipped the wine and Mr. Jones – aware of the weakness of his position since he had come by bus and had missed the last bus home – increased his offer to fifteen. His rival, however, saw more virtues in the cob with every sip he took, and his attitude hardened. 'I'll tell 'ee what I'll do.' he said at last, 'I'll drive 'ee home in the trap, and you can see how the little cob goes. Then you'll be sure to buy her.'

They harnessed up the cob and off they went. But it was very cold sitting in the trap, and when they arrived at their destination Mr. Jones naturally invited his rival in to have a glass of mangold wine.

They argued for a long time, partly about the cob and partly about the respective potency of sugar-beet and mangold. Mr Jones's rival became a trifle unsteady on his feet and Mr. Jones refused to allow him to drive home alone. So they set off again behind the stout-hearted cob; it was colder than ever; and what could the rival horse-dealer do but show his gratitude for Mr. Jones's kindness by offering him a glass of sugar-beet wine at the journey's end? And after that, of course, Mr. Jones was properly plastered, and it would have been most dangerous to let him drive home by himself.

✿ ✿ ✿

I don't know (and neither of the protagonists knows) how many times they drove that night to and fro, to and fro, between the mangold wine and the sugar-beet. They were found in the morning in the ditch, *exactly half-way* between their two homes. Both shafts of the trap were broken and the cob was grazing peacefully by the side of the road.

Mr. Jones recollects that sometime in the small hours he bought the little cob; this is definitely one up to the sugar-beet. On the other hand his rival, while agreeing that he did sell the animal, cannot remember what the price was; which is one up to the mangold. So we must admit, I think, that they finished up all square.

Farmyard Rooster

144

Field Day

I possess the photograph still: *B Coy, O.T.C., at camp, 1923.* Left wing M.P.s at that time were howling for the abolition of these militaristic organisations. So was B coy. Our faces, in the photograph, are eloquent of boredom, resentment and misery. Ill-fitting tunics sag upon sloping shoulders. Our trousers are coming down. Caps are tilted at extraordinary angles, revealing shaggy hair beneath. Due perhaps to some trick of the camera, everybody in the front row appears to be wearing enormous boots.

The only smile is upon the face of Sergeant-Major Frizell. It is a tigerish grin, bred of defiance out of despair. Our commanding officer, sitting next to him, has the glazed-eyed look of one who has attained to the indifference which lies beyond shame. I remember him as a tired cynic who taught me history and who was still suffering from the wounds he got in the war to end war. He had been twice decorated for gallantry, at Arras and on the Somme, but he nevertheless held that the last gentlemen's battle was Waterloo. His nickname, I don't know why, was Staggers.

Now upon a summer day, in the year when that photograph was taken, Staggers led us into battle. The occasion was a joint Field Day with O.T.C. of Cheltenham College. Our fervour was even less than usual because we understood that Cheltenham had a military tradition and would presumably enjoy the Field Day. We didn't like Cheltenham, and deplored the prospect of their enjoying anything. For our part, we slummocked on to the parade ground with our usual air of being Princetown prisoners let out into the yard for exercise.

In due course we deployed, upon a hillside covered with tall bracken, and by crawling upon my belly through this bracken I was able to make my escape unseen by Sergeant Major Frizell. I had some business with a solitary oak tree which I believed to harbour a sparrow-hawk's nest. It didn't, but I solaced myself by looking for caterpillars. It was a shady oak tree, and the day was hot. I decided to spend the day there. Before long, however, three officers on horseback appeared, so I shinned up the tree and hid among its foliage. The officers dismounted within a few yards of me. One wore a red hatband, and was probably a brigadier. The others, with white hat-bands, I knew to be umpires. They all lit cigarettes, and the Brigadier yawned and said "What a bore isn't it?"

One of the subalterns spread out a map and said: "You see what those Cheltenham chaps are up to, sir? They've got a couple of sections on top of the hill, to make a lot of noise and bunderbust, but they're marching their main body through this narrow valley, to take Malvern in the flank."

"If Malvern spotted them they'd be in a tight corner," said the Brigadier.

"From what I saw of Malvern on parade," drawled the other subaltern, "they looked like an outing from one of those institutions for the mentally handicapped."

I resented that. I reserved the right to despise my own O.T.C. but I objected strongly to that lahdidah subaltern despising it.

The officers rode off. I sat still until they were out of sight, and then I crawled to the end of my bough to make sure that the coast was clear. It was a point of vantage from which I could survey the whole battlefield. At the top of the hill there were white flags waving (I think they represented machine guns in action) and I could hear a lot of shouting and shots. Upon the slope below, the rumps of B Coy were visible, advancing through the bracken in a fashion about as soldierly as a herd of routing swine. Turning my head to the left I could see the valley that lay between the hills. A narrow track ran through it and up this track, purposeful as Red Indians upon the warpath, filed the cohorts of Cheltenham.

As the pattern of events was revealed to me, I gradually became interested against my will; I had an inkling for the first time of the chess game that was warfare. A signalling-lamp was winking from among a clump of trees at the bottom of the hill, and I guessed that Staggers had set up his H.Q. there. I thought what an old fool he was, to be lured into attacking those decoys on the hilltop while

Cheltenham's main force crept up on his unprotected flank. As I watched the approach of those khaki files, somehow sinister, like brown snakes wriggling up the valley, I began to think of them as 'the enemy' and I was possessed by a strong sense of impending disaster for my own side. I stood up in my tree to get a better view of their approach; and suddenly realized that if Staggers were a fool, the Cheltenham commander was even more so, for his troops were now bunched together in the narrowing valley and *they had no flank-guards out upon the slopes of the hills.* Heaven knows, I was neither by nature nor training anything of a soldier; that bird-nester and caterpillar-hunter in the oak tree was the most unmilitary creature that ever put on khaki; but at least I appreciated the dramatic nature of the situation, which was this: within 15 minutes or so, the enemy would have us at their mercy, but while those minutes ticked away they were at ours. Moreover it was given to me, and to me alone, to determine the outcome.

I swung myself out of the tree and began to run downhill towards the blink of the signalling-lamp. There I found Staggers, bored-looking as usual, with Sergeant-Major Frizell, who bristled at me like a tiger about to spring. Staggers raised his eyebrows and said:

"You look hot."

Tremulously as at attention, trousers sagging, boots disposed Charlie Chaplin-wise, I told my tale. Naturally I lied a little – I had become lost, I said, at which Frizell snorted. I didn't mention the oak tree.

Staggers' whole personality seemed to have changed suddenly. He looked about ten years younger, for one thing; he rapped out orders, he set his lamp winking again, he despatched messengers hither and thither and he actually barked at Frizell.

While all this was going on I noticed for the first time the D.S.O. ribbon on Staggers' tunic, and next to it the purple and white one of the M.C.

Looking up the hill, I saw our section leaders waving their arms and the little khaki figures running to and fro as our whole front re-formed. The manoeuvre was ragged, as were all our manoeuvres;

we shambled as we always shambled; but at least we were now facing in the right direction and Staggers had a look in his eyes as if he were imagining himself back at Arras; or perhaps with Wellington at Waterloo.

He set off up the hill, limping because of his war-wounds.

"And now," he said, "let's give 'em hell, shall we?"

And so we did. Our foremost platoons let them have five rounds rapid before they knew we were there. The range was so close that one of the Cheltenham boys was hit by a wad, which went through his cheek. His yells of pain encouraged us; and we became as Assyrians. We came down like wolves on the fold. The Brigadier, who had heard the firing, rode into the melee at full gallop; but he couldn't stop us, nor could the lahdidah subaltern, who in the confusion somehow became unhorsed. We sliced clean through two Cheltenham companies, swung 'round in our tracks, and fell upon the remnants with rifle-butts and boots. The Brigadier later praised our 'military spirit'. He didn't know that it was really a kind of furious pacifism; that we demonstrated our dislike of carrying rifles upon the Cheltenham heads and our loathing of private soldiers' boots upon their backsides.

Staggers, I believe, was told that he must 'control our enthusiasm' in future; which was like getting a bar to his D.S.O. He made no mention, in form or out, of my part in the affair; but some weeks later, during one of his cynical discourses about the Civil Wars, he suddenly glanced down at me an said;

"Posterity may treasure the initials which you are secretly carving upon your desk, but I should appreciate some proof that posterity is likely to hear of you. Have the goodness to describe to us the events which followed the Battle of Worcester."

"Er – King Charles fled, sir."

"And then?"

Staggers was looking hard at me. I blurted out;

"He – he hid in an oak tree, sir."

"Hearsay has it so," said Staggers, with one of his tired smiles; and I, even I, had the grace to blush.

When Red Admirals take over

Whenever I smell the meadowsweet I am reminded that summer's going. It's once again 'the turn of the year,' when the wild rose fades on the hedge-row briars and all over the land there's a kind of scene-shift before another act in the unending play of the seasons.

Purple or dark red is the colour motif now; loosestrife spikes by the stream sides, willowherb in the damp places, nightshade, thistleheads on the waste ground, heather on the hills.

Worn Scales

Most of the birds have stopped singing, save the repetitive greenfinch, and the lark high overhead still trickling down a small cascade of song. Soon those waste-ground thistles will shed their down, people with baskets will go mooching about the hedge-rows looking for blackberries and mushrooms.

The butterflies in the fields begin to look draggled; no wonder, since they've been dancing away every hour of sunlight for a month or more. Those meadow browns and ringlets were the colour of a good cigar when they hatched from the chrysalis. Now you can often see transparent patches in their wings where the scales have worn away.

As the marathon dancers tire and the tune gets slower the busy pipits pounce on the slowest ones. Others fall to the ground among the grass roots, where the voles and fieldmice will east them.

But a new generation of butterflies takes their place; red admirals and peacocks and tortoiseshells. A fresh-hatched red admiral is one of the most brilliant sights in nature, as it sits on a thistlehead and spreads its wings to the sun. And the yellow brimstones, just out of the quaint chrysalises that hung upon the buckthorn, look as if they had 'just come out of a bandbox' – as our grandfathers use to say.

On the posts

And this is the season when kind people are apt to bring me cardboard boxes in which, when I hold them close to my ear, I can hear mysterious flutterings and scrabble. 'Big moth,' says the proud captor, 'Found it on a telegraph pole. Never seen anything like it in my life before.'

St. Giles Parish Church,
Bredon

It's an odds-on bet that the captive is a red underwing moth, with mottled grey-brown forewings and beneath them bright scarlet hindwings which, like an old lady's red flannel petticoat, show only when the drab out covering is lifted. I don't know why these quite common moths, whose caterpillars feed on willow, are so fond of sitting on telegraph-posts. I counted 14 on 11 posts along the road near my home this time last year.

Sometimes, at dusk, I see them fluttering round the willows beside the stream which runs through my garden. The other day I watched a big noctule bat hawking among them.

The seizing of the prey happens so quickly that you're apt to assume the bat has taken it in his mouth. On the contrary, he fields it in a wing-tip, or in the 'interfemoral membrane' between his thighs, picking it up at speed in much the same way as a lacrosse player catches a ball.

Bounce back

The bat, of course, does not hunt by sight but by echolocation; as our night flying aircraft did in the last war. All the time he is hunting he emits sound waves from his larynx; these are reflected back by such obstacles as willow branches or such flying objects as moths. The computer in his brain receives the information, analyses it, and gives to his muscles and nerves the necessary instructions how to avoid the obstacle or pursue the prey.

He sends out his signals on different frequencies – sometimes as high as 120,000 cycles per second, sometimes as low as 16,000, when the human ear can just detect them. The bat's 'computer' must work pretty fast; the time between the sending of the signal through the mouth and the return of the soundwaves 'bounced back' off the prey to the bat's inner ear is reckoned in hundredths of a second.

Bowling for the Pig

The Rector is in charge of bowling for the pig. Seeds of rain blow across the Rectory orchard and the wind joggles the Chinese lanterns in the trees surrounding the lawn. They are to be lit later for the dancing if the rain stops and the wind hasn't spoiled them.

With the collar of his mackintosh turned up, the Rector is wearing the expression of an early Christian martyr. The connection between him and the god of wine is not glaringly apparent, nor would you readily associate our fete with Dionysian orgies.

Nevertheless, Dionysus, or Bacchus if you like to call him that, was the founder and originator of festivals. The word 'festival' means the same as fiesta and fete. Therefore we can assume that Dionysus presides, though perhaps with some embarrassment, over the jumble stall, the white elephant stall, and the bowling for the pig.

The bottle stall might be more to his taste. In charge of it is the landlord of our local, since the Committee thought it would be a sort of home from home for him. They thought, also, he might present some bottles. He compounded for one bottle of South African sherry, and this is the centrepiece on the table, shining like a good deed in a naughty world among bottles of tomato sauce, lemonade, chutney and Mrs. Quigly-Henderson's home-made pickles.

Each bottle has a number. The landlord has put cards bearing corresponding number into his hat, you pay a shilling for a draw, and if you are very lucky you may win the South African sherry. If you are less lucky you may get a bottle of elderflower wine, Women's Institute vintage, of which the recipient last year sipped cautiously, perceived as he thought his foolish error, and used it as hair-oil.

There are also a tea-tent and a marquee which enshrines a small flower show, there is the W.I.'s exhibition of jams and cakes, a fat pony giving rides to the children for tuppence a go, and a stall where you can buy a balloon, have it filled with hydrogen, and let it down wind in the hope that it goes to Czechoslovakia.

The balloon that travels farthest wins you ten bob, assuming that some kind person picks it up and posts it back to the Rector. It seems unlikely that a Czech peasant would trouble to do so; but a kindly Dutchman did last year. We think he believed it was something to do with the Secret Service, and that it was part of MI5's cover-plans to have it addressed to a country clergyman.

It is odd, when one considers the immense range of human ingenuity, that our little fete has the same side-shows every year, and never adds any new ones. We sit for hours at our committee meetings trying to think of new ones; but every fresh idea, upon examination, seems fraught with various moral and physical dangers, as Mrs. Quigly-Henderson points out.

Fox and Hounds

We experimented one year with a game called Fox and Hounds, for the young people, to be played at dusk. The fox was given five minutes start, and instructed thereafter to hoot like an owl at one minute intervals: the pack of young people representing the hounds hunted by sound.

But the hunt finished up in the dark wood behind the Rectory, with all the naughty girls in the village hooting like mad, and the all the young men chasing them, and the naughtiest girl of all perched on top of Farmer Pilkington's hayrick and wailing like a woman for her demon lover. It had to be stopped.

We have one innovation, however; the barbecue. Mrs. Quigly-Henderson provided a fallow-deer from her park. We overrode the objections of two local vegetarians who thought that the spectacle of a deer-roasting would be barbaric, obscene, corrupting to the children and offensive to all civilised persons. We pointed out that if this was indeed the case it might convert a lot of people to being vegetarians. They saw the force of this argument.

And now; as the rain becomes heavier and the wretched stall-holders put up their umbrellas, our local butcher, dressed as Robin

Hood (which we all think is most imaginative of him) has spitted the deer and lit the fire beneath it and already the fat is sizzling and jumping as he begins the basting. Almost all the village children are watching, and I regret to say that they do not seem to regard the spectacle as offensive and barbaric.

"No it ain't, silly, that's 'is lights."

The rest are silent, anticipatory, and licking their lips.

The loudspeaker installation is saying *Wah-wah-wah-wah-WAH*. It has gone wrong as usual. It is trying to tell people about the bowling for the pig. The pig, a small weaner with a disproportionate squeal, confined in a kind of wooden crate in the charge of the Rector, is trying to tell them too, much more effectively.

Wasps at tea

The tea-tent is full of wasps. This, too, has happened before. The bottle stall is no longer patronised because the bottle of South African sherry has been won, and the last bottle of elderflower wine handed out by the landlord with an air exactly like that of the poor Apothecary at Mantua selling the deadly poison to Romeo.

'Put this in any liquid thing you will, and drink it off; and, if you had the strength of twenty men, it would despatch you straight.'

And the jumble stall is sold out. We have made £11 3s 3d. because jumble offers an irresistible temptation to all women. Indeed we have had to make a rule that nothing must be sold from this stall until the opening ceremony is over, otherwise people arrive early and buy all the most desirable oddments.

The rain has stopped. We shall light the Chinese lanterns after all. There will be dancing on the lawn. *Wah-wah-WAH* goes the loudspeaker, trying to tell us so.

An appetising smell of roasting deer pervades the whole scene. The vegetarians look unhappy. The Rector's wife says loudly, 'Perhaps they are feeling hungry, poor dears.'

The news goes round that we have made £105 13s 6d. in aid of the Church Fabric. This is just one pound fifteen shillings more than last year. As I look around the orchard I am astonished that out of so little we have made so much.

It seemed such a silly little fete; so unfestive, unimaginative, so awfully English; and yet I wouldn't have it otherwise. It is a poor thing, but our own.

And now, as dusk creeps round us and the lanterns are lit, it is Dionysus' hour. The band plays. A few couples dance on the lawn – simply as a means of getting together. As soon as they have done so (Mrs Quigly-Henderson doesn't guess this) they go off pair by pair into the wood. Dionysus, I daresay, looks kindly upon them. He looks kindly, too, upon the winner of the bottle of South African sherry, who has drunk the lot and is singing.

'They are enjoying themselves!' says Mrs. Quigly-Henderson.

'Such a success' beams the Rector's wife. The pig squeals as its winner drags it away. The Rector, his job done, goes into the Rectory for dinner and a glass of port. He makes the old joke, 'The Rectory port – any port in a storm.' Dionysus smiles on him too; smiles on us all.

The Mice that are vanishing
from the Midlands

The delightful little harvest mouse, weighing but one-fifth of an ounce and building a charming nest amongst the cornstalks, in which it brings forth young weighing, I daresay, less than half a drachm, is probably extinct in most of our Midland counties.

I am wondering whether the dormouse is going the same way. I used to find those beady-eyed, fluffy slumberers plentifully when I was a boy, but nowadays I never come across them.

Somebody suggested to me that the gypsies eat them!

I don't believe it – they are much too small to be worth the trouble of cooking – but it is true that the Romans regarded them as a delicacy, and served them to tickle the palates of Emperors who even wearied of nightingales' tongues.

Housemice were eaten during the siege of Paris, when it was said that a chef, upholding the honour of the French cuisine even when everybody was starving, served 'roast cat surrounded by roast mice on a dish decorated with garnishing.'

❀　　❀　　❀

The author of the French 'Dictionnaire Universal de Cuisine' records a still stranger gastronomic occasion.

At the Langham Hotel, London, in 1868, three blood-horses, specially fattened, were cooked by a M. Joseph Favre, who was expressly hired from Paris. They were served to the members of the Jockey Club of all people... 'ce qui a cause un certain scandale dans la haute societe.' (Which has caused a certain scandal in high society).

A scandal in high society indeed! What would our modern horse-worshippers have to say?

❋   ❋   ❋

While I'm on the subject of food, let me say how glad I am that cheese is coming into favour again.

Until recently, the average small grocer's shop offered its customers a choice of two cheeses only, one described as 'tasty', the other as 'mild'. Both came from Canada.

Sometimes a third sort, that blue Danish which looks like gorgonzola but tastes very different indeed, was added to the list.

But nowadays the well-flavoured, dark yellow double Gloster (a better cheese even than Cheshire in my view) often turns out to be one of the grocer's most popular cheeses.

I have never possessed a whole one, which is the size and shape of a grindstone. It would be a noble sight on anybody's sideboard!

What with double Gloster, Somerset blue vinny, Leicester, Cheshire, Cheddar, Wensleydale and Stilton, we English can match our cheese-makers against the best in the world.

A Camembert, a Gorgonzola, a Gruyere, might be as good as one of our best Stiltons – but it would have to be the best that the foreigners could find.

We hardly deserve our good fortune, since our hearty barbarians not only muck up their Stiltons at Christmas by pouring into them beer, stout, or port wine, but actually boast of this bestiality!

Ask any of our Midland makers of Stilton what they think of the application of beer or wine to their beautiful cheese, then beware of the consequent explosion!

❋   ❋   ❋

The other day I climbed to the summit of an outlier of our Cotswolds – Meon Hill, north of Chipping Campden.

Alone on the top (where some bent and evil-looking crab-trees sighed to themselves in a high, hot, thundery wind) I bethought me uncomfortably of the murder which took place there eleven years ago.

An old man, having not an enemy in the world, nor any possessions that would tempt a thief, was battered to death on the hilltop where he was trimming a hedge. His long-handled hedging tool was used to pin him to the ground, being driven like stake through his chest.

No murderer was discovered – or (as far as I know) suspected.

Men in the bar of the pub at nearby Quinton, who are extremely unwilling to discuss the affair because it is eerie and discomfortable and jolly near home, say that there was a similar murder on Meon Hill 100 years ago.

If so, it suggests all sorts of possibilities – imitation witchcraft, ritual murder, and so on.

Can anybody tell me if there is an account of the earlier murder published in any antiquarian's history or contemporary newspaper?

If it really happened in the1850's there surely should be plenty of documentary evidence.

Home in time for the Flower Show

It is pleasant to go abroad now and then but it is doubly pleasant to come home.

The night before last I was drinking cognac and singing a Burgundian song about the gathering of the grapes with a barman whose home is at Nuits Saint George. But to-day, in contrast, I am involved in what I suppose, is the most typically English activity of all, the village flower show.

❈ ❈ ❈

"So you got home safely?" says Frank, my gardener, as if we had been to Timbuctoo.

"Yes."

Then he tells us the news. My wife and I have only just arrived at the show, and the car, still full of luggage, is parked outside the village hall.

"We got a first for roses, and second for long carrots, but our parsnips wasn't so good."

❈ ❈ ❈

They never are. To win a prize in our show parsnips have to be almost four feet long.

You bore a great hole with a crowbar, fill it with suitable fertiliser and plant your three seeds at the top of it. When they germinate you choose the likeliest seedling and pull up the other two.

Your pet parsnip then proceeds to bore its way down towards Australia.

It is very nearly a day's job to dig it up, because the last six inches of delicate root are liable to break away unless you carefully remove the earth from round about them with a teaspoon.

The product of all this labour is a very interesting botanical specimen, but is no more edible, I imagine, than a horse-radish.

(The above remarks should be read, of course, in the context of the preceding paragraph. "Our parsnips wasn't so good." Hence the sneer at all parsnips which win prizes. Witness, gentle reader, how a man's character begins to deteriorate as soon as he goes in for competitive gardening!)

※　※　※

Inside the village hall everything is the same as it was last year, and the year before, and the year before that. The judges with their grave faces, as serious as if they sat on some international tribunal, the enormous vegetable marrows, the cauliflowers like heaps of snow (and Mr. A. muttering to himself that he shouldn't be surprised if Mr. B. bought his in a shop); the tight round cabbages, like green footballs, the leeks like young palm trees, the stupendous onions that have been twelve months a-growing, the dear little nosegays of wild flowers gathered by the hot sticky hands of the schoolchildren; the jars of honey, the apples glossy as horse chestnuts, the little clutches of hen's eggs as golden brown as the sands of sables d'or which we left only 48 hours ago.

※　※　※

We are back in a world where the little daily things are important: the sort of world which Gilbert White lived in when he set down meticulously in his immortal chronicle the day in every year when the children of Selborne first played hopscotch on the village green: the sort of world of which Miss Mitford told, of which Cobbett's children wrote to him when he lay prison, because he had asked them to let him know every detail of what happened on his Hampshire farm.

"The corn is in good ear in the Ten Acres, the spaniel bitch has had four pups, the Aylesbury ducklings weigh four and a quarter pound in the feathers…"

I am sorry for any man who finds no delight in such little things; because three-quarters of our lives are concerned with them.

"And Scarlett's kittens have just got their eyes open..." It was a pleasant and very English welcome home.

※　　※　　※

And now, as I stand admiring Bill Barnfield's chrysanthemums, the secretary of the flower show comes up to me.

He says "I wonder if you'd mind judging the Ankle Competition at the flower show dance?"

O blessed, glorious, comical, complex England, with its prize parsnips and its ankle competitions, its vegetable marrows tuberous as fat sows, and its jam jar of wild flowers plucked by the hot sticky hands of Gloria Jones, aged eight.

Beloved, ridiculous England, it is nice to be back!

Garden bridge over the Squitterbrook,
Lower Mill Farm

Talking at the top of his Voice

I have been re-reading, as every countryman should do from time to time, Cobbett's *Rural Rides*. What a boisterous book it is! And how the wind blows through it, that blustering wind of Cobbett's great spirit which seemed to blow him along all his life!

He was 50 when he wrote *Rural Rides*: he had a bright red face with white hair atop "like snow on a berry." During the 50 years he'd left behind him he'd done a vast number of magnificent and foolish and extraordinary things.

He'd "run away from the plough," joined the Army, become a regimental sergeant-major, taught himself to write (and corrected his officers' grammar in the Regimental Orders); he'd married a dutiful wife and had nobody-quite-knows-how-many children; he'd been compelled to flee twice from England, once from America, and once from France; he'd had his windows broken by angry mobs in places as far apart as Philadelphia and London.

He'd been fined for libel, imprisoned for sedition, and made bankrupt; he'd quarrelled with half the world, but most of all with the village parson; he'd farmed big and small farms in England and America; he'd edited newspapers, published hundreds of pamphlets, and written books on such diverse subjects as French Grammar, horse-shoeing, making bread, brewing beer and keeping bees!

※　　※　　※

He did none of these things by halves. When he libelled a poor wretch called Dr. Rush in America he attacked the doctor's powders and politics in seven successive issues of a newspaper, then brought out five numbers of an entirely new paper called *The Rushlight*, which was devoted entirely to abuse of Dr. Rush and finally he wrote a pamphlet *libelling the Chief Justice who fined him for the original libel.*

❊   ❊   ❊

Then take his prejudices. They were enormous and absurd prejudices; he hated tea, potatoes ("a noxious weed"), religious tracts, girls' schools, the *Times* newspaper, flannel underclothes (which his wife insisted on wearing), stock-jobbers, puritans, Milton, Shakespeare (whom he summarised as "bombast, puns and smut"!) and most of all King George IV, of whom he wrote with satisfaction on the day after he died, "I can find no good thing to speak of, in either the conduct or character of this king."

He was a violent, energetic, egotistical, inspired, glorious ass; but of course he was very much more than that. Re-reading his book, I found myself seeing him as an expression of the English spirit; he stands for our stupidity as well as our wisdom; for our pugnacity, generosity, obstinacy, our follies as well as our good sense, our love of freedom, our hatred of injustice: all our virtues and all our faults, compounded and magnified in him!

For example, although he was essentially a Radical (and a very Left-wing one, as we'd say today) he was also intensely and violently patriotic. If the British Government was to be beaten over the head – which it jolly well deserved – then *he* was the man to do it; but if any foreigner dared to interfere in his private quarrel, so much the worse for the foreigner!

For instance, when Cobbett flew from the wrath of King George and settled in America he bought a bookshop and decorated its window with a large portrait of the King. The mob smashed his window for that; but the English Radical had shown where he stood.

❊   ❊   ❊

His *Rural Rides* is a book, somebody said, of a man talking at the top of his voice. He shouts for joy about good ploughing, pretty girls, a pack of foxhounds, well-bred cattle, Wiltshire cornfields, great oaks, a field of swedes, a crop of maize, which he called Cobbett's corn.

He roars with anger about the Rotten Boroughs, the "whiskered gentry," about the poverty of labourers, about tithes and parsons, of which even the black-coated rooks eating the wheat painfully remind him.

For old time's sake he rides out of his way to the Botley parsonage and bellows and cracks his whip under the parson's windows; but Mr. Baker will not budge and Cobbett rides away disappointed.

With all his foolishness, he is quintessential England. Like Mr Greenwood in 1939 he "speaks for England." He does more than that; he shouts, he hollers for England.

And whether he's right or whether he's wrong we cannot but love him, nor feel but that England would be the richer if she possessed a few such as he in these politer days.

Farm hay wagon

The Tongue-tied 'Bumpkins' live in the Cities today!

Some boys from the city, spending a camping holiday nearby, came down to the tench-pond where I sat waiting in vain for a bite.

They ranged themselves along the bank on either side of me and, since they weren't getting any bites either, they talked to each other *across* me, discussing their private affairs with as little concern for my presence as if I had been an old heron watching for fish.

The subject-headings of their conversation (mainly feminine) have no place in this article; what did shock me was their extraordinary poverty in words, their very real difficulty in communicating more than the simplest sentence, their utter lack of any glimmering of imagination, compared with country boys of similar social class.

This is surely an odd reversal; it was *our* folk who used to be the 'bumpkins.' It was Hodge, the stolid farm labourer, who was supposed to be tongue-tied, communicating painfully by means of "Eh's" and "Ar's." The quicker-witted townsman was the fluent one.

✸   ✸   ✸

I got the impression, however, that these town boys had a basic vocabulary of only 300 or 400 words, a child's portion, indeed it sounded even more limited than that, because they always attached the same dull swear-word to every noun!

What was the cause of the trouble? A worse education in the city than in the country – again a reversal of the precious trend? Or TV, gooped at hour after hour, day after day, until its addicts become morons with emasculated imaginations? Or the idiotic baby-talk rock'n roll lyrics?

This may indeed be the answer. In Ireland recently, where there is no TV in the countryside, and no queer addiction to rock 'n roll, I was struck by the beautiful, free and imaginative speech of even the poorest peasants, who called surprising similes to their aid and used a quaint and unexpected imagery, describing a skittish horse, for example, as "leppin' into the elements."

❈   ❈   ❈

The country speech of Gloucestershire and Worcestershire, despite the TV, is still quite lively, though less so than in the days when everybody went to church as a matter of course on Sundays.

When even humble folk were familiar with the Collects, and the Authorised Version, a kind of reflected light, a glow and splendour, was shed upon their talk and upon the letters which, however laboriously, they wrote with much better 'education' than is generally demonstrated today.

The glory of the English language, and especially the toughness and vigour of its youth, was preserved and kept alive through the Bible.

And though the Bible's influence on our speech is gradually disappearing there is still a trace of it in country places where a middle-aged man is likely to have learned his first words and phrases from a father and mother who, through hearing the lessons read each Sunday, was familiar with the noblest English, other than Shakespeare's, that pen ever set down on paper or parchment.

❈   ❈   ❈

But these boys from the city – alas, they who had received a much more expensive education than their fathers had – who had stayed at school longer – and for whom the best books had been provided free and without stint – were unable to communicate even with each other save by means of a few score monosyllables and a dozen or so disyllables so distorted and truncated that they sounded like the grunts and croaks and snarls of a primitive, perhaps even of a Stone-age, Tribe!

*The John Moore Countryside Museum,
Tewkesbury*

Country Causerie

What a poem could be written on the theme of English place-names! Indeed one could make a lyric for every single sheet of the one-inch ordnance map, singing such words as Windrush and Evenlode, Bablinghythe, Saint-Mary-in-Roseland. But there are quaint names, too, which would lend themselves to such comic metres as the limerick: Wig-wig, for instance, discovered by one of my companions in a *Sunday Out* broadcast near Much Wenlock last week.

What dull fellow seeing a signpost to Wig-wig, would not feel compelled to visit it? Mr. Michael Rix, of course, could not resist it, and so discovered that Wig-wig consisted of not much more than two cottages and a water-splash. Still, he has been there; let others boast of their visits to the Victoria Falls or the Taj Mahal. He has been to Wig-wig.

And I, as I drove through Radnorshire the other day, discovered a mountain called the Smatcher, which lies in the neighbourhood of two little places named respectively Evenjobb and Hurlingjobb. The Smatcher is as round as a hay-tump but steepish, and 1,396 feet high; a delicious little mountain.

But what is a Smatcher, pray? What is the meaning of the verb 'To Smatch'? Lewis Carroll might have invented it. It might be inhabited by a Bandersnatch.

Elan beauty

I was on my way home (when I encountered The Smatcher) from fishing at Rhayader, from casting my flies, fruitlessly alas, in the water which perhaps you people of Birmingham will be drinking next week. Those huge dams in the Elan Valley always make me doubt whether hydro-electric schemes and such-like really do 'spoil the countryside,' as they are generally supposed to do.

In the Elan Valley man has not merely changed the landscape, he has created a new one; and it may be a lovelier one than was there before. You look down now and then from that steep mountain road on a scene of breath-taking beauty; and the great dams themselves in no way detract from it, for they seem almost as solid and enduring as the rugged mountains which rise about them.

I have never seen such colours in a mountain country as I saw during my drive back from Rhayader. There were hills which the gorse, in full bloom, had turned into fabulous mountains of gold, purple and green. There were rowan trees so thickly berried that they looked like blobs of scarlet.

There was one field of over-ripe wheat in a valley which glowed in the sunlight, and seemed almost to smoulder, so deep a rust-red that I could scarcely believe it was a field of corn. Three buzzards, a raven, a peregrine and lot of dippers with their clean white bib-and-tuckers completed my happiness on that unforgettable afternoon.

Nameless

And then, when we stopped for a drink at a little pub in a village which must be nameless, I enquired, as I generally do, about the local fishing and received the delightful reply: 'We don't do much fishing with the rod-and-line hereabouts; *groping* and *snatching* is more in our line, look you.' And my wife, in superb and sublime innocence, looking wide-eyed from one man to another asked gravely:- 'Are groping and snatching legal, then, in these parts?'

There was a moment's awed silence before the seven old poachers, and the landlord as well, burst out into such a simultaneous yell of laughter as I daresay had never been heard in that pub before. They were completely and joyfully shameless.

They vied with each other to tell two perfect strangers how they caught salmon with gaffs and grappling-hooks and rabbit-snares; how they tickled trout; how they fished with night-lines, with salmon-roe, by every illicit means; how they had caught a six-pounder only last season, under the bridge at the end of the village street, using of all things a large lump of cheese.

'And are there no water-bailiffs?' I couldn't help enquiring.

Dark thought

'If you ask me,' said the oldest of the men, 'the water-bailiffs iss the worst of the lot. Not a good word can I say for the water-bailiffs. Their business takes them down to the river at night, do you see? And what do they get up to, do you imagine, in the hours of darkness?

'If you ask me' – he lowered his voice – 'If you ask me, sir, them water-bailiffs iss nothing but a pack of damn poachers?'

Shakespeare's Birthplace,
Stratford upon Avon

Nowt so good as
Withybobs' in September

'At this time of year, you wants to fish with withybobs,' so said
the Old Man of the Weir in the days of my youth. He had a long
black tarry punt in which he would carry you across the Severn,
for a fee no greater than that which Charon charges to ferry you
over the Styx – to be precise, one penny. But you couldn't rely
upon him to bring you back!

An angler might come along and then it would be: 'Take you
fishing, Mister. Show you all the best places, bob an hour for the
boat and your bait chucked in, and if we makes a good bag you
wets my whistle at the Lower Lode Inn.'

I don't think he often went dry; for he not only knew the best places, he provided the best baits. If it was the season for red worms he'd go and dig with his horny hands, rather as a mole digs, in the warm sticky refuse of a rotting rick.

Lobworms he caught on his own little lawn at dusk – "You creeps up behind them and you cops 'em by the tail."

In June he always collected a kind of waterweed off the Weir which he called 'Rate', it was a good bait for chub. And at the appropriate seasons he'd bait your hook with elvers, or grasshoppers, or little frogs (as Izaak Walton cruelly recommended), or blackberries, or elderberries, or stewed wheat, or rank cheese, or wasp-grubs, or the pith from an ox's marrow got from the butcher's.

❈   ❈   ❈

But withybobs? 'Nowt so good as a withybob to catch a chub in September.' He promised to show me some and we hugged the bank, drifting downstream while he scanned the willow-branches.

'There you are,' said the Old Man of the Weir at last, and he nosed in to collect from an overhanging bough a whole nest of the gregarious furry tallow-speckled caterpillars of the Buff-tip Moth.

He baited my hook, and with the first throw I had a three-pound chub which came for the withybob open-mouthed, making a considerable bow-wave with its big blunt head.

Four-pounder

That afternoon, even allowing for the five per centum per annum interest which Memory adds to the avoirdupois of fishes, I reckon I caught sixty pounds of chub – including one four-pounder. We landed him just under the marl cliff at Wainlode, which presumably was long ago a wagon-crossing of the Severn, between Tewkesbury and Gloucester.

'Allus get a good fish here,' said the Old Man of the Weir with satisfaction. "Allus plenty of fish here, allus will be. Look 'ee at that cliff. I've heard tell as it's made of fish-bones. Allus fishes here, even afore the Flood."

❀   ❀   ❀

I don't know which Flood he meant; I doubt if he did. But he was right about the cliff at Wainlode. As long ago as 1842 a geologist discovered the fishes. The cliff, I should explain, is composed of layers of limestone, shale and marl.

Where the tea-green marl joins a layer of black shales near the top of the cliff there is the 'bone-bed' which astonished the Victorian naturalists; for fish-fossils are never very common compared with the more durable molluscan shells, corals and such-like.

Fish tombs

These black shales, however, proved to be the tombs of millions of fishes; when you split them open you could see the forms of the scales imprinted within them with the bones and jaws in innumerable teeth.

These fishes swam about 150 million years ago – a little time (as geologists measure them) before the sea retreated and the Dinosaurs waddled in the swamps it left behind.

But my Old man of the Weir knew nothing of Dinosaurs, and 150 million years meant no more to him than a couple of hundred. 'Allus fishes here, even before the Flood.' And nobody can dispute that; yet I think that if you fish at Wainlode tomorrow you'll be more likely to catch a chub than a coelocanth.

Farewell, Swallows – Hail to Autumn

Our beloved swallows which nest in my mare's stable will soon be off; so will our house-martins which build their 'procreant cradles' (Shakespeare's lovely phrase, not mine!) under the eaves just below our bedroom window.

We have watched the little heads with the large demanding mouths poking out from the nest holes, and the ceaselessly busy martins flying to and fro with flies. Our cats have often sat on my wife's dressing-table and watched too, in hungry frustration; but there's no conceivable way in which they could get within reach of the martins.

As usual, there's a late brood of swallows in the stable; the babies not yet fledged. This is a drama that happens almost every September; our improvident swallows presumably did not notice, a month or so back, that already the days were drawing in. Very soon now they will have to make the agonising decision, whether to stay behind when their companions start the migration, or whether to go with them and abandon the babies.

Survive

The issue is never in much doubt, I think. Nature's command to all her children is urgent and unequivocal: SURVIVE! So the parents fly away, and the baby swallows squeak and whimper for a surprisingly short time before they die.

'It turns your tummy over,' my wife says, when the restless migrants gather on our single telephone wire 'to think of such little things setting out on that awful journey' – across the turbulent seas and the trackless deserts and the jungles which look like green foam as you fly above the tree tops – I know, for I have been an aviator, too!

I have no idea what the casualties may amount to, what proportion of those setting out will reach their destination – in some years I think the losses must be staggering. Last Spring only two pairs of swallows came back to us, whereas we usually have six or eight. They arrived late and exhausted, and one bird died on arrival.

Wiped Out

Swallows, of course, are so plentiful, and are such quick breeders, that these migration casualties do not affect their numbers in the long run. But a rare species can be nearly wiped out by some ill-chance such as an errant depression in the Atlantic, a sudden unexpected change of wind.

Farewell, swallows; farewell martins. They are the last of summer. When they are gone, however bright the sun may shine, we shall know we're in autumn.

Dewy mornings have a nip in the air, and the muck-heap 'smokes,' a little white mist hanging over it as the hot moisture rising in vapour condenses in the cold.

Autumn's with us; winter round the corner. But I would not have it otherwise. I always find myself looking forward to the next season just before the last one has ended. Coleridge, who wrote that lovely line; 'Therefore all seasons shall be sweet to thee' – wrote also a note in his diary concerning these changing seasons and his delight in them; 'Every season Nature converts me from some unloving heresy.'

The Song of the Swallows
is gone from the Land

We have said goodbye to our pet-particular swallow, which we noticed first 18 months ago because his tail-streamers were much longer than those of his fellows.

Perhaps, indeed, they were too long; for when he returned to us last April he was one streamer short – possibly some predator, just missing him, had carried off part of his tail?

I cannot make a guess whether or not he'll come back next year; the casualty rate must be pretty high during that 3,000 mile there-and-back journey.

Meanwhile, we miss his merry twitter from the single telephone wire outside my study, where he used to sit. It's a charming little song, the swallow's; a kind of happy *tirra-lirra* such as Sir Launcelot sang by the river, according to Tennyson.

The martins have left with the swallows; indeed, I think the two birds often fly together, in mixed flocks, over the deserts and the forests and the seas.

'Delicate air'

Both kinds honour my house and its outbuildings, which suggests, according to Banquo in 'Macbeth,' that 'the air is delicate' here!

> *This guest of summer,*
> *The temple-haunting martlet does approve,*
> *By his love-mansionry, that the heaven's breath*
> *Smells wooingly here; no jutty, frieze,*
> *Buttress nor coign of vantage, but this bird*
> *Hath made his pendant bed and procreant cradle;*
> *Where they most breed and haunt, I have observed*
> *The air is delicate.*

He spoke to Duncan; who was to find Macbeth's castle less hospitable than the martins did –

Macbeth: Duncan comes here tonight.

Lady Macbeth: And when goes hence?

These I suggest are the best and the most terrifying two lines of dialogue ever written, just over eight words and your hair stands on end.

※ ※ ※

But to get back to the martins; 'pendant bed and procreant cradle' is a marvellous description of those mud-plastered, cosily-lined nests hanging under the eaves. Shakespeare knew his birds, as he knew everything else!

He loved them all, I think, from the wren, 'the most diminutive,' 'with little quill,' to the swift, beautiful falcon with which Othello compared his Desdemona before jealousy quite drove him mad –

If I do prove her haggard (that is to say wild, untamable)
Though that her jesses were my dear hear-string
I'd whistle her off, and let her down the wind
To prey at fortune.

The jesses were the leather strips fastened round the legs of a hawk, by which the falconer could hold it. But what a phrase it is – "I'd whistle her off and let her down the wind."

I can never see a windhover hunting but I think of it. And what a name is windhover for the kestrel which hangs motionless with its blunt head in the very eye of the wind!

※ ※ ※

One cannot write of Shakespeare's birds without remembering the rollicking nonsense of the song in 'The Winter's Tale' –

The white sheet bleaching on the hedge,
With heigh! the sweet birds,
O! how they sing!
Doth set my pugging tooth on edge;
For a quart of ale is a dish for a king.

The lark that tirra-lirra chants,
With heigh! with heigh! the thrush and the jay,
Are summer songs for me and my aunts,
While we lie tumbling in the hay.

Let anyone who thinks of Shakespeare as "solemn scholars' stuff" dons' reading dull examiners material – let him contemplate those last two uproarious lines, and think again!

A corner of Tewkesbury Abbey

Seeking a Hobbly 'Onker Champion

Now comes the season of mast and nut and acorn. The spiny green horse-chestnuts come thumping down in the churchyard to the delight of small boys who hope to find within one of them the hobbly 'onker champion, the Kinkering Konk.

The beautiful beech-trees shed their mast, the mahogany-coloured three-cornered nuts of which that kindly botanist, the Rev. C. A. Johns, wrote; "They're much appreciated by squirrels and children."

Bitter

I used to nibble them, when I was about six, but I don't recollect that the nuts were very agreeable and my impression is that they were nearly as bitter as the acorns which we also tried to eat – perhaps for the sake of the fun we had in peeling them, removing the exquisitely graven chalice, splitting the skintight, hard green rind.

I suppose they must be nutritious; pigs grow fat on them and in Spain and North Africa certain starveling humans feed on the acorns of the allied holm-oak.

And did not the Germans grind them up to make a substitute for coffee which they could no longer import during the two world wars?

❊　　❊　　❊

The hazel's harvest is the best of all. Boys still go 'nutting' and bring home basketsful of the elf-capped brown hazels which, when they are properly ripe, are as tasty as the Kentish cobs, though much smaller.

I'm often asked what is witch-hazel, and whether it too bears nuts. It doesn't; and in fact witch (wych) hazel is just another name for the witch (or wych) elm.

Some say that 'wych' comes from an old word meaning 'pliant,' and has nothing to do with the tall-hatted ladies who ride the skies by night; but the experts in words come down on the side of 'wych' being merely another spelling of 'witch,' and the tree having some supernatural significance.

A water diviner generally uses a twig of witch hazel – again, I suppose, because of its magical associations. Would not an ash or willow twig serve his purpose as well?

❋   ❋   ❋

Personally I don't believe that the wand has anything to do with the finding of water.

A lot of people are going to get very cross with me about this! But I am not saying that water-diviners cannot find water. I am sure they can. You could hardly drill a well anywhere in England without find water!

The truth of the matter is, I think, that the successful 'diviners' are simply expert practical geologists, whose skill in summing up the geological features of the terrain tells them where is the best place to dig – although for all I know they may believe their power is supernatural and may react to that belief with an involuntary contraction of the muscles at the moment when they think they are passing over the most propitious spot.

Hocus-pocus

What I cannot bring myself to believe is that 'earth-currents' or electro-magnetic impulses (which have never in this sense been proved to exist) can produce the contraction in the muscles of some men and not of others; or that they can act direct upon a twig and make it jump, in some hands and not in others.

This seems to me sheer hocus-pocus; as do the claims which some diviners make that they can find hidden treasure and the bodies of murdered people and perform other such witcheries.

The Moods of a Tree

There is a willow grows aslant a brook
That shows his hoar leaves in the glassy stream;
Whenever I see a willow-tree that leans over like that I think of
poor drowned Ophelia. I think it is one of my favourite trees, but
its very name is sad, say it aloud to yourself, but softly, and it is
like an unrequited lover's sigh! This the makers of songs well
know. O willow waly! they cry; and
> *All around my hat*
> *I wear the green willow,*
> *All around my hat*
> *For a twelve-months and a day,*
> *And if anyone shall ask me*
> *The reason of my sorrow,*
> *I will tell them that my true love's gone*
> *Far, far away!*

❈　　❈　　❈

But not all willows weep. Some dressed in Lincoln-green in the
late spring, have a lightness and a grace that makes one think of
maidenhood; other, old ones, at winter twilight are like ancient
hags, witch-like, malevolent, holding up crooked arms in
supplication, warning, despair.

No other tree, I think, has so many moods. I love it, and
delight in its infinite variety, though it hasn't the grandeur of the
great Forest trees. I believe the botanists can differentiate and
name with long names several score of species and sub-species;
but this seems to me an unremarkable achievement, for the poets
can differentiate ten thousand.

No willow is like another willow. Walking beside the little
River Stour at Shipston the other day, I came across a row of very
old ones, so ancient that their trunks had split, and some of them

were bifurcated and seemed to stand upon two legs like gnarled old men, and some even had three legs and reminded me of those horrible thinking-vegetables of the future which I read of recently in an ingenious thriller, *The Day of the Triffids*.

But somehow or other their roots survived and got some sustenance from the soil; and in turn they gave sustenance to other plants and trees which had seeded themselves in the leaf-mould and rotting wood which filled some of the space between the splits in the trunks.

Miniature gardens and, indeed, miniature shrubberies grew there; willow herb, loosestrife, groundsel, dog-rose, sycamore, hawthorn, privet, even little nut-bushes with a good crop of nuts on them growing, almost as if they had been grafted there, out of the tops of the trunks of those ancient willow-trees.

As an amateur naturalist I love willows, not only for themselves but for their parasites. Exciting caterpillars inhabit them. In the rotten wood you find the big, hideous grubs of the goat-moth, which burrows in the wood and chews it into sawdust, living there for more than two years before it turns into a great grey moth.

Goat-moth grubs smell like goats. (Dr. Johnson would have disapproved of that slovenly sentence. Being reproved by a lady, 'Dr. Johnson, you smell,' he replied unrepentantly; 'No, madam, you are wrong. You smell: I stink.') At any rate, it is possible, when you stand to windward of a goat-infested willow-stump, to identify the caterpillars by their smell.

Then there are puss-moth caterpillars, and eyed hawks, and the caterpillars of red under-wings which, when they turn into moths, always remind me of old women with red flannel petticoats; for their forewings are drab, brown and grey, and it is only when they lift them that you suddenly see the black-hemmed, bright scarlet of the hindwing underneath.

For me there is no end to the fascination of willow-trees; for the fattest trout always seem, to lie beneath them and it is always a ticklish cast, sideways, left-handed (and how often into the teeth of the wind!) – but if one catches that difficult trout he will seem to be worth half-a-dozen easy ones!

And one more virtue of the willow, which I nearly forgot, is of course that it was devised planted and nurtured by a far-seeing Providence for the express purpose that its specially-resilient wood should enable Messrs. Hutton, Graveney, Compton and co. to delight us by whacking a leather-covered ball over the smooth turf of fields called Trent Bridge, Headingley, Old Trafford, Lord's and The Oval!

Fox and Hounds,
Bredon about 1952

Seasons of Mists – and Anger

A notice scrawled on a blackboard outside a shop caught my eye: *Wanted 100 tons blackberries, wanted damsons 75 tons.* This is very different from last year, when the blackberry-pickers had a thin time and it was almost impossible to give damsons away. About this season I walked up a very quiet valley in Shropshire which was extra-quiet somehow, which had an indefinable air of decay, and all around me, for acres and acres, there were drooping, overladen, damson trees, heavy with rotting fruit. Every orchard was slate-blue with damsons. But nobody had picked them, and nobody would pick them.

I encountered one farmer (the only human being I met during that desolate walk up the valley near Morville) and I was tactless enough to mention damsons. The valley ceased to be silent. At the top of his voice he told me what he thought about damsons, and the dealers in damsons, and an ungrateful country which no longer wanted to stew damsons, or to make them into jam, or into wine, or into pickles, or to extract a purple dye from them as once it did.

'Damn damsons!' he roared. 'They call this place Damson Valley' – and then quite softly he added: 'They say it's very pretty in the spring when the blossom's out…'

But you ought to have heard his tone, the dreadful quiet ferocity with which he said 'they say it's very pretty in the spring…'

I left him at that point, and turned back down the valley road, and read on the gateposts the notices which ran; Messrs So-and-So regret that owing to the jam manufacturers 'low price and the high cost of chip baskets and picking they cannot buy any damsons this year…'

❈   ❈   ❈

And all the orchards were still, where there was usually such a chatter of pickers, and all the trees were broken by their large, useless burden of the bitter bellyaching fruit.

However, it's an up-and-down trade. A few men made fortunes out of damsons during the war, and this year the orchards will at any rate show a profit. For my part I have no use for the sloe-like things, save when my wife pickles them in vinegar and sugar in a big earthen jar. Then, after two years or so, they are delicious and are the perfect accompaniment to that cold roast mutton we have been given the opportunity to get tired of...

❀   ❀   ❀

I have been in Herefordshire, where the harvest of course is of hops, and I have been talking to the pickers about a piece of bureaucratic nonsense which makes me hot with rage. School holidays (eight weeks) occupy the period from the end of July till early September. Hop-picking, however, is in full swing for the whole of this month.

If the pickers bring their children they are fined for their children's non-attendance at school; but in most cases there is nobody to look after the small children if they leave them at home. Therefore the pickers (mostly miners and their families from the valleys of South Wales or workers from the Black Country) must either deny themselves a profitable and healthy holiday or put up with a summons on their return.

Most of them choose the summons; they are then fined a pound or two, and in Wales at any rate they refrain from paying the fine until a warrant comes for their arrest.

Why must we be so inflexible? Why not *either* alter the time of school holidays in the districts where hop-pickers come from *or* accept the fact that a fortnight or three weeks in the Herefordshire hopyards is more valuable to any brat than the same period spent at an overcrowded school in Dudley or Pontypridd?

❀   ❀   ❀

I have hardly ever seen happier children than those innocent law-breakers. A few of them pick hops; indeed they do so very enthusiastically for the first two or three days; but after that they play in the sun, among the green glory of the bines. They eat better food, with better appetites, than ever they do at home: and they pick up, if they are old enough, a little knowledge of how country people live.

Are schoolteachers so arrogant as to believe that 'lessons' are the only valuable things to be learnt? And are bureaucrats so rigid that they never go out of their offices and study this problem in the field – that they never go to the hopyards and learn from Mrs. Dai Jones of Aberdare and Mrs. Smith of Tipton why they sometimes defy the law in order to give their children a good holiday and themselves a bit of a break.

※　　※　　※

It is all part of our absurd, 20th-century idea that everybody must be treated alike: that individual needs, individual hardships, simply don't matter. What is best for all must be best for each. But why? We are all different.

We have different pleasures, hobbies, ambitions likes and dislikes. We are all *persons*. We are not just numbers and names.

I read a long bureaucratic report on 'Human Relations in Industry' the other day. The horrid word *Personnel* appeared 47 times. Isn't the whole trouble – in industry and everything else – that we have ceased to think of workers, managers, shop-stewards and clerks as *people*. We call them *personnel*; and once we do that we forget their individuality.

The lack of flexibility in the enforcement of our school-attendance laws is the direct consequence of this attitude. X wants to take his family to Blackpool in August; Y wants to go hop-picking is September. It simply demonstrates the stupidity of our educational bureaucrats that they are incapable of arranging matters to suit both.

My Old Mac

My Uncle Tom, may he rest in peace, believed in boys starting at the bottom; and literally my first job as an auctioneer's clerk was to stick the numbered tickets on the behinds of cattle as they heaved and horned in a milling mass at Upton-on-Severn market.

For this purpose I wore a filthy old mackintosh indistinguishable from the filthy old mackintosh on one of the market porters, a disreputable fellow called Tommy Hodges.

When I had finished labelling the cattle I joined another lad called Stanley and together we 'clerked' the sale.

We stood beside the auctioneers while they were selling and recorded each transaction upon slips of paper; then we took our slips into the little market office and spent four hours or so doing sums as quickly as bookies' clerks have to do them, 35 tegs at 63s 6d, 15 hens at 2s.11d, 19 store cattle at £9.15s.6d, and so on.

All the time we were taking cash, giving change, making out receipts, chi-acking with drovers and farmers, and even writing out the cheques for those who could sign their names but 'had no book-larnin!'

There was no till in the office; we were a curiously old-fashioned firm; and we simply stuffed the cash and cheques into the pockets of our mackintoshes, crumpling fivers up with cheques for £500 in a lordly and casual way.

At the end of the day we rode back from Upton-on-Severn to Tewkesbury, the two of us on an old Douglas motor-bike, and proceeded to balance our books.

We were never allowed to go home until they did balance; and although we sometimes stayed in the office till ten or eleven at night, we never failed to get the figures right, even though a big market in those days involved a turnover of three or four thousand pounds.

Now I have said my old mac was exactly like the market porter's old mac; and one day as I went to have a wash before setting off home I hung up mine beside his behind the door of our little office.

When I came back I took the wrong one by mistake, jumped on the back of Stanley's motor-bike and we rode off to Tewkesbury.

When we got there I put my hand into the pocket and pulled out, instead of the wad of cheques and money, a thick bundle of betting slips which T. Hodges, who acted as a bookie's runner when he wasn't working for our firm, had collected from his customers.

I stared with horror at the filthy scraps of paper inscribed with such cryptic sentences as *5s e.w. Gay Lad Hurst Park 2.30*: and I realised that T. Hodges was wearing my mackintosh with some three thousand pounds in it.

My uncle, fortunately, was not in the office, so we crept out, got on the motor-bike, tore back to Upton and began to draw the pubs, systematically, for we knew that T. Hodges would be in one of them.

He always got drunk on market day, but we knew that his method of drinking was that of the butterfly rather than that of the camel. He took no long draught anywhere, but sipped here, sipped there, like a Red Admiral on the buddleia bush.

So we hunted him from the White Lion to the Anchor, from The Crown to the Coach and Horses, and so on.

✻   ✻   ✻

There were in those days, I believe, some 27 pubs in Upton-on-Severn, and we had visited 25 before we caught up with T. Hodges, whose custom it was to drink a half-pint at each.

His twenty-fifth half-pint had overcome him. He was sitting alone in a dark corner, snoring. On his knees lay the mackintosh. In the mackintosh pocket, in cheques, notes and coins, was three thousand seven hundred and twenty-three pounds, two shillings, and eleven pence.

I laid his own mackintosh upon his knees, but he slept soundly, and as we went out of the pub into the street we could still hear the diapason of his snores.

Back in the office we counted the cash, hurriedly added up the long columns in our ledgers. It balanced, first time, to a penny.

My uncle came out of the back room where he worked just as we were preparing to go home. 'What? Balanced already, boys? Quick work. Well done!'

And neither he nor, oddly enough, T. Hodges ever knew.

Gypsy caravan

Caution at Cowfield

I read in my local paper that they were going to make a children's playground out of Cowfield Meadow.

For my part, I had never thought of it as anything else. There were always children playing there when I was a child. Cowfield might have been designed by the Almighty expressly as a playground for small boys and girls.

The farmer grazed a few cows there, with which we lived at peace.

There was a narrow, winding stream in which grew yellow water-lilies that we called brandybottles, because they were supposed to smell of brandy (which we had never smelt – otherwise we should have known differently!).

Fell in

Reaching out over the stream to seize them with a crooked stick, we sometimes fell in. The brook was shallow, and we came to no harm.

There were green and silver fishes, called bleak, which lay near the surface on hot days and allowed themselves to be caught by any child old enough to catch a bluebottle fly, impale it on a hook, and dangle it before their noses.

For bigger boys, for the kind of expert anglers we became by the time we were 12, there were shy chub, perch, and small pike which could be noosed with a rabbit wire hung on a willow-wand.

Just in case we should ever grow tired of this delightful meandering stream there was also a pond, in the very middle of Cowfield, where we caught sticklebacks which built nests in our improvised aquaria, and newts like miniature dragons whose passionate and uninhibited courtship we observed with awe.

There were also whirligigs and water boatmen, big shiny water-beetles and the fierce-looking larvae of dragonflies, frogspawn to which we likened our loathed tapioca, tadpoles in the spring and the little tiddleywink frogs that jumped and plopped around the margin of the pond in the summer.

Stolen

All round the pond stood ancient willow-trees, cloven by time, so that you could squeeze yourself inside one and hide there.

You could also climb out on one of the stout boughs which overhung the pond and look down, not only upon the newts and waterbeetles swimming there, but upon a minute rushy island where moorhens, unbelievably devoted or stupid continued to build nests and lay eggs despite the fact that the eggs were generally stolen.

But the most climbable tree of all was a big oak in the centre of Cowfield, which had low spreading branches and foliage so thick in summer that by the time you'd climbed ten feet up it you were as well hidden as King Charles.

All round the edge of Cowfield lay a tangle of dewberry and blackberry bushes.

But we boys weren't very interested in blackberry-picking. We used the bushes as cover in our complicated games of cowboys and Indians.

When we tired of these games we played cricket upon a pitch which had been hammered out by the feet of generations of boys.

You were out if you hit the compo ball into the blackberry bushes. But it was six for a swipe into the brook, and by tradition the bowler was the one who had to wade in and retrieve the ball from among the lily-pads and the watercress.

But they are making a playground out of Cowfield Meadow.

Already they have bulldozed the blackberry-bushes and the willow and filled in the pond. (Children might fall in, children might get their feet wet!)

For the same reason they're going to fence the little stream.

Shortly they will put up all over Cowfield those peculiar structures which you see on playgrounds nowadays and which I fancy were designed by a committee of gym-mistresses, child-psychologists and safety-first experts.

Here the children will be able to swing and slide and 'express their personalities' without the least danger.

Indeed already I see that they have started to build some little towers of tubular scaffolding which look rather as if they belonged to Whipsnade, where kindly keepers perhaps contrived them for the exercise of clambering chimpanzees.

The rates

After all, you've got to give children something to climb....

The acorn tree? Oh, they cut that down because daring boys might climb too high and fall and break their limbs.

Then perhaps there would be an action against the Council, and the damages would go on to the rates, which get higher and higher all the time, what with the cost of making playgrounds and things.

The Big Feed

Now on hillside and in hollow, along the hedgerows and the headlands, in the woods and at the ditch-sides, in patches of waste land and at the bottom of your own garden, all manner of small creatures are making frantic preparations against the cold which creeps on apace.

The squirrels pile up their hoards of hazel nuts and beech mast, the jays along the edge of the oak wood bury acorns by the score (and being jays shortly forget where they buried them).

Most of the bats have gorged themselves fat on the last of the flies and have hung themselves up in belfries, eaves and hollow trees – though the pipistrelles, which are light sleepers, will sometimes launch themselves forth on a mild evening in midwinter to prey on the gnats which dance in the lee of the hedges.

The hoarders-up of food – I mean the creatures which, like squirrels, pile up their little private stores – are few and far between.

Most animals, and especially of course hibernating ones, realise that the best way to store their food for the winter is in their own tissues. Their aim during these late autumn days is to eat and eat until they are as plump as it is possible for them to be.

The foxes are fat, and the badgers are fat under those rough rugs which serve as their fur coats, the little field mice and the voles are probably the fattest of all.

Our cats know this. This is their hunters' moon.

The little teeth of the voles that have been chewing so busily during the past month or so have in a sense been doing the cats' work for them, producing plump little barley-fed voles, more tasty than they are at any other time of the year.

Goodness, the little hedgerow mice are busy! The other day I happened to pass in a gateway a pile of those plastic bags in which fertiliser is now delivered.

The farmer had been using them to carry crushed oats on which he was feeding some young cattle. When they were emptied a few oats remained in them.

As I went through the gateway, I was aware of a peculiar loud chirruping; and when I examined these bags I found they were all of them inhabited by long-tailed field-mice which had got inside and for some reason or other were unable to find their way out.

There must have been three or four mice in each of the bags. So I held the bags upside down and shook them out and they scurried away in twos and threes with their long tails whisking.

※   ※   ※

The late butterflies have already sought out their winter hiding places. Brimstones generally shelter themselves in the cracks of old trees; the small tortoise-shells often hide in houses or garden sheds.

So do the red admirals, but these, I think, never survive the English winter, though they always *try* to hibernate.

That is to say they feed themselves fat on the last sweets of the flower, seek a comfortable shelter, fold their wings over their backs and go to sleep.

But during this slumber, the deeper everlasting sleep creeps upon them.

Many entomologists have tried to overwinter red admirals but I do not think any have succeeded unless they have provided very artificial conditions for them.

But why, you say sensibly enough, do the red admirals not die out in England if none of them survives until the spring?

The answer is that our stock is renewed by immigrants from Southern Europe which appear in the early days of the spring.

Not very many of them, but enough to lay their batches of eggs on the nettles and produce a second generation of red admirals, which we see on the thistle-heads and buddleias during August and September.

194

❋   ❋   ❋

Scores of butterflies and moths, beetles, flies and other insects hibernate in the cracks of bark, in the debris at the foot of trees, deep in the evergreen bushes and so on.

Many other sorts hibernate as caterpillars (which often come out on mild nights to have a bite of anything green that's going).

But most of the butterflies and moths spend the winter as chrysalises, sometimes in their well-tailored silken cocoons, sometimes lashed to a twig or a leaf with a silk girdle, sometimes buried underground at the foot of the trees.

❋   ❋   ❋

Already the little mice, and such of the hedgehogs as have not yet gone into hibernation, are on the look-out for these caterpillars and chrysalises, whose fatty tissues will help *them* to fatten up against the winter.

And the birds are busy too, probing with their beaks among the grasses, searching the bark crevices and seeking among the dead leaves.

But the birds take much less trouble than the other creatures to prepare themselves against the coming cold.

Those that have not adapted themselves to our winter climate have wings that will carry them across the seas.

I think there is no winged bird that hibernates anywhere on the face of the globe.

Down where the Cider Apples grow

Olde Foxwhelp, Strawberry Norman, Dymock Red, Slack-my-Girdle; do those names mean anything to you? Probably not; they were given long ago to certain sorts of apple – mostly bright scarlet, small, hard and extremely sour – out of which the farmers in the West Country used to make their cider.

There was another kind called Black Taunton which had a dark red skin and pinkish flesh and was used in small quantities for the purpose of colouring the cider.

During the war, when the price of eating apples was controlled at 12s a box, you could get 12s a box for anything you sent to the wholesalers; and our less scrupulous farmers even sent off their Black Tauntons, which doubtless looked pretty on some spiv's barrow.

God help the poor innocents who bought them, though! They are so sour that if you take one bite you suffer for some time afterwards a curious numbness of the gums – as if you had had an injection at the dentist's.

The rough cider, or as we call it 'scrumpy,' which is still made by a few farmers with these and other kinds of cider-apple, got itself into the news recently, when Dr Tewfik, the consultant psychiatrist for South Worcestershire, issued a statement to the press about the incidence of alcoholism in the Vale of Evesham.

The shakes

He said that about a third of the patients in a local mental hospital were alcoholics.

'It is really very unusual. I believe it is the rough cider that is doing it. If you drink it at the rate of six pints or more a day for a number of years you are asking for trouble. First you get the shakes....'

You do indeed; though I shall probably be drummed out of my village for saying so! Some farmhouse cider is about four times as strong as ordinary bitter beer.

Six pints of cider equals 24 pints of beer! And our old-fashioned cider drinkers don't stop at six pints a day.

I know a chap who used to drink TEN pints a day, which he increased to 12 after his wife died – when he got into the way of taking a quart bottle home to have a swig at if he should wake up in the night and feel lonely.

I knew two old cronies who drank so much cider that they fell into a kind of second childhood together, and were seen one Sunday evening after closing time standing unsteadily outside the pub and solemnly playing hobbly-'onker with their gold watches.

RIP. They've gone the way of all flesh, thanks to Slack-my-Girdle and Strawberry Norman, Old Foxwhelp, and Dymock Red.

Unprintable

We have various names for this strong rough cider which is still regarded by some as the national drink of Gloucestershire and Worcestershire. Some of these names are funny but unprintable.

Tanglefoot and Stunnem are the polite versions, sometimes used in court.

"'Ad a few pints o'Tanglefoot, your worship, and got into a bit of an argument with a chap...."

Certainly our locals aren't very particular what goes into the cider press. A man to whom I sold the fruit off a small orchard of cider apples and perry pears some years ago waited until the windfalls were brown and mushy, then gathered them up with their attendant slugs and grubs and moribund wasps, and made them into scrumpy.

He told me that he added "a bit o' pig's liver and a bit o' good beefsteak" during fermentation, and that "the cider were kind o' hungry like, the beefsteak was yut up in no time."

He was good enough to give me a small barrel of this cider, which seemed to me undrinkable. I put it in an outhouse, where it worked away for two or three years yutting-up any remaining horrors which in his experimental fashion he'd put into it, and one very hot day the roadman came our way and cut my grass verges, so I asked him if he'd like to try a drop of real cut-throat cider.

He enjoyed it so much that he came back every few weeks and turned the grass verges in our lane into the likeness of a lawn.

Then one day as I came back from the village I saw a leg with a boot on it sticking up out of our ditch in the way one saw legs and boots after a battle in the war... but the roadman was still alive, snoring steadily, a beatific expression on his face, and the cider cask was empty, not a drop left!

Stocks at Stow on the Wold

The Squitch Fires bring
the Scent of Autumn

Soon it will be squitch-fire time. 'Squitch' is the country name for couch-grass, one of those weeds which it's no use burying – you must dig it out of your ground and burn it with the other rubbish; so autumnal bonfires are all called squitch-fires!

They burn with a blue smoke that spreads along the hedges and looks like a mist of late September.

They tickle the nose with a tang half-sweet, half-bitter, which goes with the smell of damp dead leaves to make up the quintessential, indescribable smell of autumn.

But of course all smells are indescribable, save by comparison with other smells. Whereas we can describe things seen by their colour and shade, things heard by their tone and pitch, rhythm and air, our noses lack vocabulary; we can say a smell is sharp or sweet or that it reminds us of geraniums or the seaside, but that's about all.

Nostalgic

Yet a smell acts upon the memory more powerfully than anything seen or heard. It will extinguish 30 years in a fraction of a second; and transport you, let us say, to a childhood daisy-bank where you wove your first daisy-chain at the age of four.

The scents of plants seem particularly nostalgic. Each one has for me some special significance of time and place, whether it be primrose, hyacinth, honeysuckle or the clear smell of the first mustard and cress I grew on a wet flannel!

❋　　❋　　❋

To return for a moment to our squitch-fires, it is remarkable how just a few of them can give a tang to the whole countryside, which hangs about for days.

This reminds me that the very first smells which men became aware of were those caused by burning; for the word 'smell' has its beginnings in the ancient word for 'smoulder' and 'smoke'.

There was a time when fashionable folk preferred the more polite Frenchified 'perfume'; but now perfume has become the most 'non-U' of all 'non-U' words, and the people who set store by such silly conventions will be frightfully shocked if they hear you say 'perfume.'

Actually this is one of the few 'U' conventions which seem to make sense to me, because 'perfume' is a very affected word and quite un-English, like the word 'commence' which used to be the pet affectation of people who thought 'begin' was a bit vulgar.

Posters

But nowadays nobody says 'commence,' except perhaps the auctioneers, who in their posters perpetuate this out-moded refinement: 'The sale will commence at 11 o'clock precisely.'

❈ ❈ ❈

Words are as subject to fashion as women are; they are always getting out of date or coming into fashion again unexpectedly. In my native town of Tewkesbury I still hear people speaking of a 'boughten' cake; but your middle-class housewife calls it a 'bought' cake, and would be quite shocked by 'boughten.'

All the same, that sturdy past-participle was good English once, and is good American still. I like it, for it has a strong Anglo-Saxon sound, like 'beholden', which country people still use frequently when they are being splendidly obstinate and defiant; 'I won't be beholden to nobody.'

A good English sentiment to set down in good ungrammatical English terms!

The Colonel who caught a Pied Mole

The other day my neighbour found an 'albino' hedgehog: the first I have ever heard of, although all hedgehogs are whitish when they are first born and their spines are soft as hairs.

But this hedgehog of my neighbour's was fully grown, and he described it as 'biscuit-coloured' – what women call beige.

He tried to confine it until he could show it to me: but hedgehogs are expert gaol-breakers and it managed to get away.

I should have liked to see it, for hedgehogs are the least variable of mammals: 'Sports' must be rare among them

Moles on the other hand wear coats of the most unusual colours.

The old whisky-drinking Colonel whom I have often written of, and who taught me much natural history when I was a boy, was a great catcher of moles.

He had an ambition to have a moleskin coat made for his sister, and had worked out that it would take 250 skins.

Proud

But the moles on his farm were more various than other people's; and he was very proud of this eccentricity.

Now and then, instead of the usual grey-black pelt with its pewtery sheen, the coat of his captive would be yellow or sandy, the colour of a Tamworth pig.

He swore to us one day in the pub that he had seen a pink one ("and that was long before I took to drinking dam' near a bottle a day").

But his greatest find was a pied mole, part sandy, part black.

He brought it to the Swan one evening, pulling it out of his horrible haversack which had a most peculiar smell, due to its being coated inside with assorted feather and fur, dried blood and the encrusted slime of fishes.

'Clean'

There were two compartments, one reserved for 'clean' things, i.e. non-slimy ones, because it was also the receptacle of his lunch-time sandwiches.

Upon this particular occasion, when half the Colonel's haversack was filled with half a dozen eels which he had caught for his supper, the other half, the 'clean side,' happened to be hopping with fleas which had come off a hedgehog he had saved from a dog.

It also contained two plover's eggs which he intended to cook for his breakfast and some assorted wild flowers which he had picked because they were the first of the spring and he wanted to show them to us.

Routing about among these he fetched out at last for our inspection his last exhibit of the day.

It was this pied mole, the head and shoulders black, the rest sandy; rather like a Wessex saddleback in marking. And of course, it made the Colonel more proud of his moles that ever.

'Pretty little beggar; never saw the like of him in all my days. Well, he'll make no more oontitoomps on my lawn.'

Roads

To go back to hedgehogs. I have never seen so many killed on the roads as I have seen this autumn.

It is amazing how the hedgehog population maintains itself despite the autumnal slaughter.

Don't ask me why so many hedgehogs wander about on the roads at night, especially at this time of year: I don't know, and I believe nobody knows.

The casualties are always highest just before the hedgehogs go into hibernation. I counted seven dead ones the other morning on a five mile stretch of second class road where the traffic at night is never very heavy.

A Danish biologist estimates that 120,000 hedgehogs annually are run over on the roads of Denmark.

On this basis we might make a guess that the number killed in the United Kingdom each year is 750,000; but I should not be surprised if it was higher.

❋ ❋ ❋

The shrews, whose bodies are found in such numbers at this time of year, die of natural disease or old age, I think; I have often counted a dozen at the roadsides during a county walk.

The other day in this column I wrote about the pygmy shrew, a creature no bigger than my thumb, and I observed that it was the most quarrelsome, aggressive and ferocious of our mammals.

By chance only a week later I came across two of these shrews fighting in our lane. The battle went on for several minutes before they tumbled together into the ditch, after which I lost sight of them.

Often, I am told, they fight on until one or the other is killed.

Ferocity bears no relation to size. Indeed the most aggressive snakes are the small ones; and of all our birds the fiercest fighter is certainly little Jenny Wren.

On the other hand, my neighbour's red poll bull which weighs I daresay three quarters of a ton, is the most peaceable creature you could hope to meet.

Out shooting, as I crouched behind a hedge waiting for partridges, he walked up unbeknownst to me and snuffled down my neck...

His name – a most odd one for a bull – is Leprechaun.

When Sparrows are 'Wuss'n the Rabbits'

I have never known such a plague of sparrows. During the harvest they rose in clouds round the edges of the barley fields – from a distance they looked like a continual brownish smoke blowing about there.

For about 10 yards into the fields from all the headlands they had taken their tithe of the corn; in places they must have reduced the yield considerably.

"It is wuss'n the rabbits," one farmer told me; and privately I think he was wishing for a sort of myxamatosis of sparrows.

Long poles

In the old days, at this time of year, the boys would go 'batfowling,' with nets carried on long poles which they placed at night against the ivy growing on a wall.

They would shine a light on the ivy and the 'Dick Spodgers' that were roosting there would fly out in alarm and become entangled in the mesh of the netting.

In this manner they would sometimes catch scores of sparrows in a night. Later they would pluck them and roast them on spits over a fire. The sparrows were fat after harvest time and the breasts were 'better than chicken.'

'What have you been eating?' their parents would ask, when they noticed the grease shining on chin and cheek.

'Poor man's pheasants!'

More plentiful

Maybe the batfowling boys controlled the sparrows to some extent. Today everybody agrees that the birds are more plentiful than they used to be.

In the spring they descend in droves from the barn where they live and rip the flowers off my polyanthuses and crocuses (for some reason they prefer the yellow ones always).

Later they make confetti out of the fruit buds.

My peas are under continuous assault from the moment the seeds chit to the time when the pods are ripe. I can't grow lettuces unless I cover the rows with wire guards. In the autumn the sparrows amuse themselves by ripping open the green sheaths of the sweet corn to get at the cob.

Humanitarian

I suppose one could lay all this at the door of the admirable Royal Society for the Protection of Birds! It's a measure of the success of the society's propaganda that the kind of boys who carry coshes and bicycle-chains tear up flowers in public parks, shoot out people's eyes with airguns and slit each other's gizzards with jack-knives nevertheless regard a sparrow's life as sacred!

At any rate they don't go batfowling nowadays; not even the most bloodthirsty of them. Or perhaps it's simply that they've got worse things to do...

The trouble is that I too am becoming more and more humanitarian so that I cannot bring myself to take arms against the feathered hordes, as one acquaintance of mine has been driven to.

He blazes away at all kinds indiscriminately declaring that as he's not a 'Hopping Hornithologist' he can't be expected to distinguish good from bad, common from rare.

Thank Heaven for our Autumn Colours

The poplars now sprout up like golden fountains. The sycamores' bright flame is of a rounder shape; where big sycamores stand alone they are splendid roman candles.

Theirs is, I think, the richest yellow, with a touch of orange in it.

Their close cousins, the maples, show scarlet as well, but not to the same extent as the genuine sugar maples of Canada do.

Their scarlet, especially if you see it against the dark pines, is matched only by the red of the sumach trees, which incidentally, are grown in so many of *our* gardens now that they brighten up the suburban autumn tremendously.

Each deciduous tree fades in a different fashion and produces a different shade.

Stand at the edge of a mixed woodland at this time of the year and you will see every colour from palest yellow to deepest red. Even purple.

Some of the big hawthorn bushes go wine-coloured before they shed their leaves, and the clumps of buckthorn which you find along the sides of most mixed woods turn to a most marvellous shade of reddish-purple damson colour.

❀　　❀　　❀

Everywhere surely, the oaks are the loveliest. Their yellow makes a marvellous contrast with the sepia branches.

In the sun they always make me think of old oil paintings, and especially paintings which have not been cleaned – Gainsboroughs perhaps.

But when the light fades out of the land at dusk, or before the sun colours things up at dawn, then I think these oaks look just like old woodcuts, and I think of the beautiful engravings which Bewick made.

※　　※　　※

Ash and willow are unspectacular, fading very gradually from green to a sort of dirty lemon tint.

The elms go blonde in patches like the girls you sometimes see in southern Europe, natural brunettes whose brown hair grows too quickly into the dyed blonde!

Elder makes a fine yellow, though it does not last long; the leaves fall away quickly as soon as the frosts come.

The horse-chestnuts have a prayerful look as each long digit droops down resignedly.

Then a wind comes, and the leaves spin away, revolving goodness knows how many times before they reach the ground.

They must be the heaviest of the falling leaves, surely. You hear them hit the ground with quite a plop on a wet day.

If ever I think of autumns in my childhood I remember the horse-chestnut leaves piled high above the conkers which we were hunting for in the churchyard. I remember their cold caresses against my bare knees.

※　　※　　※

There is a great variety nowadays among the shrubs which we grow in our gardens, and some of these are making a wonderful show along the outskirts of towns.

The flowering currant goes a splendid red, and so do some of the viburnums.

Liquidamber colours up marvellously; some of the dogwoods, especially the variegated ones, display delicate pinks among their green and silver.

As I write this, the most charming tree in my garden is an *Amelanchior Canadensis*, turning through all the shades of orange and tawny to delicate pinkish red.

The *brightest* red, incidentally, better than any maple, is the American Red Oak, which I planted right in front of the house so that we can see it from the sitting-room windows.

For 11 months of the year it looks no different from an ordinary English oak, but see it in the fall!

I suppose the colour is carmine really, but the brightest carmine you ever saw – blood red. There is a quotation from Hamlet which fits my American Red Oak at the end of October:

Head to foot
Now is he total gules.

❈　　❈　　❈

For contrast not far away stand some white poplars.

Alas, they are falling now, but in recent days, whenever the wind has blown, they have tossed their flowers of silver into the air most prodigally, catching the sunlight with a glint like new-minted half crowns.

❈　　❈　　❈

As for the chemistry of it, I have no knowledge at all.

By what metabolism the chlorophyll that made the leaves green changes into something which dyes them yellow, or scarlet, or purple is a mystery into which I have never enquired.

I am content to thank heaven for deciduous trees.

How dull to live among the unchanging spruces of Prussia or the dull green firs of Scandinavia, or the blue gums of Australia (lovely as they are), which look just the same in January as they do in June.

...*and the Weather still rules the World*

"'Tis not the husbandman," wrote Thomas Fuller long ago, "but the weather that makes the corn grow."

The husbandman, of course, has his answer to this.

It is neatly put in a story about an old man who had taken over a patch of waste land and after a couple of years of hard work had made it grow good crops.

As he was working upon it one day in late September the Rector came by and leaned upon the gate. He admired the excellent kidney beans, the onions and the marrow.

'It's Harvest Festival on Sunday,' said the Rector. No doubt we shall see you at church, for it is very fitting at this time of year that we should all together thank God for His fruits of the earth which He helps us to grow.'

'That's as maybe, Rector,' said the old man, 'but you ought to have seen this bit of ground when God had it on His own.'

Unaware

We are coming to the end of what is surely the best year that our farmers have had (from the point of view of climate and crops) for a generation.

Townsmen in the nature of things are probably unaware of this; it is unlikely to affect their livelihood in any dramatic way, though I suppose in the long run it will be reflected in the balance of payments: the more we grow ourselves the less we have to buy from abroad.

But in a modern industrial state the ups and downs of agriculture no longer spectacularly affect the economy.

A disastrous drought or a severe frost might put up the price of the vegetables at our greengrocer's but we should be unlikely to feel the pinch in our standard of living.

Whereas, if the cities of Coventry and Birmingham alone suddenly failed to sell their motor cars in the United States the consequences would be apparent very soon in the Bank Rate, in taxation and indeed over the whole economy.

We should all be tightening our belts as a result of it.

Pegged

These reflections are occasioned by my reading an extremely interesting book, 'Seasons and Prices, the Role of the Weather in English Agricultural History,' by Dr. D. L. Jones (Allen and Unwin, 28s).

It has made me realise how feather-bedded we all are by comparison with our ancestors a hundred or two hundred years ago.

Then every farmer, every countryman and most townsmen were directly at the mercy of the weather to a greater or lesser extent.

A summer's drought meant small hayricks and precious little winter feed; there was little or no importation of feeding stuffs from abroad.

So when October came, the drought of the previous summer began to make itself dramatically felt upon the whole of the nation's economy.

In the first place the price of meat went down as the farmers hastened to send to market the sheep and young cattle which they knew they wouldn't be able to feed during the coming winter.

Then very soon the price of meat went up as meat became scarce – then scarcer – then almost unobtainable.

Hostage

I shall return to this interesting book in a 'Country Column' later.

Meanwhile, I cannot resist a quotation or two from the Annual Summary at the end, in which Dr. Jones gives a picture drawn from contemporary documents of the weather in relation to agriculture in all the years since 1728.

It makes one realise how great was the husbandman's hostage to fortune in those days; how precariously every man's livelihood and, even in the case of a poor man, his life itself, depended upon the clemency or the unkindness of the elements.

For example, in 1740, after a winter of 'unheard of' frost a late spring and a cold summer, the price of wheat was *trebled*; 1748, on the other hand, was 'a year of plenty... a very fine harvest and bread never cheaper... a great plenty of everything else.'

In 1762 'a summer of unparalleled drought' had the usual effect of first reducing then raising the price of meat, but the hot weather also produced a vast crop of acorns which' induced the raiser to fatten and kill their whole stock of hogs.'

So you could have bacon and pork for a song in October but a poor man wouldn't be able to afford it between Christmas and the next summer.

Stunted

In 1795 east winds stunted the wheat; untimely frosts in June caused thousands of new-shorn sheep to die of cold, the harvest was late and small and the yield was a fifth less than usual.

In my native town of Tewkesbury 'a mobb – mostly women'- looted the sacks of flour lying on the quay, the Riot Act was read to them and some of them were tried at the Assize and sent to prison.

Nowadays most of us live our lives much further removed from the consequences of bad weather; but let us not kid ourselves that in the long run it is what comes out of the ground that is the foundation of the whole world's economy.

With a world population that is going to double itself within thirty years, we should forget that at our peril.

Before you wage War on the Worm...

Among the new chemical pesticides about which the Council for Nature expresses some concern (it is not sure how much harm, if any, they do to wild life) are two compounds called Chlordane and Toxaphone.

It is not thought that they are very harmful but they are used for the purpose of killing earthworms on lawns and the possibility exists that the birds might eat the dead earthworms and be affected by the chemicals.

The lovers of closely shaven lawns are always getting worried about earthworms because, of course, their castings show when the grass is cut nearly as close to the soil as a man's beard is shaven close to his face.

I think the English are the only people in the world who go in for this type of lawn.

Lush and green

Americans use the rotary cutters that leave about one or two inches of grass – as indeed, I do myself.

My lawn looks lush and green most of the time. The last thing I want it to look like is the wicket at Lord's or a bowling green.

So, for my part, I am very happy to let the earthworms live.

As Darwin discovered more than 100 years ago, they are useful little creatures. Mankind wouldn't get on very well without them.

They spend the whole of their lives digesting organic debris such as dead leaves or grasses, later excreting the residue in the form of castings.

Three jobs

They do three useful jobs simultaneously. Their little workings of burrows aerate the soil, their castings provide valuable humus, and the organic matter contained in them helps the soil's fertility.

Where the soil is fairly rich there are generally about 26,000 earthworms to the acre and these little burrowers, as industrious as (and much more useful than) moles, collectively distribute about 15 tons of humus per annum on the surface of the soil.

Fifteen tons! Try to work that out in wheelbarrow loads and see if you would like the earthworm's job in an acre of garden.

I have known gardeners who actually buy earthworms at so much per thousand for the purpose of improving their poor soil.

Worm breeding

Worm breeders, of course, also sell to fisherman. I am told there is a considerable market for those little red worms called brandlings, and for the 'gilt-tails' which you find sometimes under the manure or in your compost heap.

I doubt if anybody breeds the lobworms which are also in demand by fishermen. I used to catch them when they were half-way out of their holes in the evening just after the lawn had been watered.

The lobworms were very shy and I had to wear gym shoes, otherwise they heard me coming. ('Heard' is perhaps the wrong word; they were aware of the vibrations.)

Having seized hold of the worm, the difficulty was to ease the worm out of its hole without breaking it in two. Had it broken, the odds are that both segments would have regenerated and there would have been two worms instead of one.

That is one of the advantages of being a worm.

Six feet long

To return to your lawn; at least give the matter a thought before you decide to get rid of your earthworms. Ask yourself if they're really doing you any harm.

For, as I have pointed out, they are very useful little animals and in England at any rate nobody need be alarmed by them.

In Australia it is a very different matter. The biggest earthworm in the world, which lives in Queensland, measures six feet long. I shouldn't like to find him on my lawn.

And in New Zealand, I am told, the Maoris consider their earthworms to be a great delicacy and devise all sorts of ways of cooking them.

There are some kinds which are considered so luscious that they are allowed to be eaten only by chiefs.

Snowshill,
Gloucestershire

We never loved Romeo but...

One of the hens went broody – and my provident wife hates to 'waste' a broody hen. That is why our garden is populated by such an extraordinary assortment of land and water fowl: Poland bantams with fuzzywuzzy topknots, 'silkies' like two-legged powder-puffs, and on the stream a variety of ducks – mallards and mandarins, pochards and Carolinas. Most of these came from eggs which my wife bought because she did not like to contemplate the unhappiness of an unfulfilled broody.

This time she presented the hen with six silver pheasant eggs which cost five bob apiece. Five chicks hatched safely and were brought up by the maid-of-all-work Rhode Island, who in previous seasons had mothered some Aylesbury ducklings and a brood of guinea-fowl. Life could have few surprises left for her; if she'd hatched out a roc or a dodo, I think she would have been quite unmoved.

When they were about half-grown the silver pheasants left her and took to roosting in the low boughs of an elder-tree. Soon there were only two left; the others had been eaten by Sammy Davis Junior, one of our cats. We never actually saw Sammy with a pheasant in his mouth, or even so much as a pheasant's feather on the tip of his nose; but we could tell by the way he looked up at the elder-tree whenever he passed by it that he had killed and eaten those three young pheasants. He simply could not resist looking up at the well-remembered bough; yet you could see that he was embarrassed at being seen to do so.

We swore and growled at him whenever he went near the elder-tree; so that he became ashamed of himself and left the two surviving pheasants alone. We were naturally delighted, when they grew up, to discover they were a pair, and we called them Romeo and Juliet.

Alas, they were star-cross'd as their namesakes; indeed, in all the feathered tribe from wren to eagle I doubt if there has ever

215

been a bird unluckier than Juliet. She suffered a fate as rare and remarkable as that which a friend of mine rather boastfully recorded in what he called *A Ballade of Notable Decease: My great-aunt's niece's governess was run over by a TANK!*

The decease of poor Juliet was just as notable, violent and bizarre. On a hot day I was slumbering full length in a deck-chair on the lawn. Unknown to me, little Juliet had crept under the chair for shade. I am somewhat accident-prone concerning deck-chairs and I suppose when I put this one up I had failed to fix it securely. It collapsed. My weight is not inconsiderable, and Juliet died.

It was shortly after this tragedy that Romeo's very forceful personality began to assert itself. One day I saw Sammy Davis Junior in full flight, with Romeo hard on his brush. The bold bird chivvied the other cats too, and made my mare shy when he flapped at her in the drive like some bird of ill-omen from an overhanging tree. He would fly at human beings if he did not like them, and he conceived a sinister passion for pecking at bare legs, especially the bare legs of little girls.

We put all this down, in the modern psychological way, to his being turned against the world by the early death of his bride and the grotesque fashion of it; and a kind friend, being told the sad story, presented us with a silver pheasant of his own, called Miranda. She was a very quiet, grave little bird who suffered from some congenital lameness. Despite this, she faithfully followed Romeo as he strutted round the garden, dragging herself after him even if she were tired out. Every now and then the beastly bird would turn round to see if she was there; and finding that she was, would peck her sharply two or three times.

He took to wandering far afield, down the lane and into the village. Miranda, who was frightened of cats and cars, refused to accompany him on these expeditions. But Romeo was frightened of nothing under the sun. On the first few occasions when he appeared in the village, kindly people would ring us up and say that we ought to go and catch him – 'They were afraid the cats might get him, else.' Within a few days it was quite a different story; they were ringing up to ask us to rescue their cats from Romeo.

Then he took to holding up cars like a highwayman. Once he stopped the Rector's car, defying the Rector to run over him, and holding him at beak-point, as it were, for ten minutes, when he was on his way to a carol service.

That was at Christmas time. Soon the weather sharpened, with snow on the fir-trees where Romeo roosted. Their branches overhung the lane, and Romeo from his snowy eyrie glared balefully down upon passers by, human or feline. Miranda always sat at a respectful distance from him upon some extremely uncomfortable branch. – Romeo saw to that – exposed to the east wind. She was obviously terrified of Romeo, but looked up to him in awed admiration of his tyranny; as perhaps Fraulein Braun looked up to Hitler.

Spring came, and with it the young lettuces, peas and early cabbages in cottage gardens. Romeo strode up the rows and took what he wanted; ripping up any plants that he didn't want to eat, just to show his power. By now he was a real despot and looked like one; he had the beaky mad look of a Roman Emperor, and if anybody opposed his merest whim he would display the temper of a frustrated Nero. A poor old woman trying to protect her seedlings against him went for him with a broom. He flew at her in such a fury that she dropped it. She dared not stoop to pick it up; and seeing she was weaponless, Romeo ruthlessly drove her before him, step by step into her cottage. He then resumed his destruction of her single row of lettuce.

We had to do something about it; confine him or give him away. We had a sneaking admiration for him still, and we did not like to think of him captive behind the poultry-wire. We therefore tried to find 'a good home' for him in some less populous place, where he might be allowed to keep his freedom but could do little harm. We found one such 'good home' but within a week his new owner was on the phone to us begging to be released from the bargain; she spoke darkly of 'troubles' – about somebody's cat, about somebody's broccoli, about somebody's small daughter's legs... .

So Romeo was given away once more and this time there was no agreement that he should remain free. He was confined in a very large run with twenty White Wyandottes and his mate Miranda; and there was a vague promise that we would be told how he was getting on.

Months later, during another cold spell, the telephone rang.

'It's about Romeo...'

'Yes?'

'A terrible thing... One of us must have left the hen-run gate ajar... Too much Christmas dinner, I daresay... During the night a fox got in there...'

Lower Slaughter,
Gloucestershire

218

We had never *loved* Romeo but one couldn't help admiring him. If he was Roman in his tyranny, he was also Roman in his pride. It was disagreeable to think of the mean little red assassin cornering him in the fowl-pen, creeping closer and closer…

'There was blood and feathers everywhere. It was horrible. Every single one of the Wyandottes had its head bitten off. And poor dear little Miranda…'

She would crouch down before her assassin just as she cowered when Romeo pecked her, accepting what came as her proper punishment for having done something wrong and to make matters worse not knowing what it was that she'd done wrong…

'And Romeo?'

'Oh, *Romeo* was all right… The only living thing left, strutting about the pen, looking pleased with himself…'

We might have guessed it! The vanquisher of all the cats in Kemerton, holder-up of the Rector's car – what would he care for a mere *fox*? I could imagine him red-eyed and terrible, pacing the pen in his unpleasant springheeled way, gorgeous tail held proudly behind him, awful and arrogant as ever, fee, fi, fo, fum – foxes, cats, clergymen and motorcars, little girls' legs, all come alike to him: the magnificent and deplorable bird.

Birdlime that caught People

The rose-red yew berries have a translucency; the pale sun shining through them lights them up. Wrote Walter de la Mare:

Of all the trees in England,
Oak, Elder, Elm and Thorn,
The Yew alone burns lamps of peace
For them that lie forlorn.

The birds have had most of the berries by now.

It was once believed, according to old Gerard the herbalist, writing about 1630: "If birds do eat thereof it causes them to cast their feathers and many times to die."

Not crystal clear writing but you can see what he means!

"Moreover, they say the fruit is dangerous and deadly unto man, and if any doe sleepe under the shadow thereof it causes sicknesse and oft times death." Gerard went on; and with an almost schoolboyish glee declared it was all nonsense:

"For when I was young and went to schoole, diverse of my schoole-fellowes and likewise myself did eat our fils of berries of this tree, and have not only slept in the shadow thereof, but among the branches also, without any hurt at all, and that not one time, but many times."

❂   ❂   ❂

Of course he was right. I know. Because as a kid I fairly gobbled the petty red yew berries and came to no harm at all. We all did.

I and my young friends were a pretty experimental lot, at the age of 12 or so. We believed in trying everything once; and we never had anything worse than a tummy-ache in consequence.

But the yew berries were sweet and innocuous. I said so on the wireless, a few years back, and got into frightful trouble. Parents, doctors, learned botanists wrote to the B.B.C., which had to broadcast a warning to children *against* eating yew berries.

Apparently I was right about the pink pulp of the berries, that was quite safe; but the *stones* could poison you.

It never occurred to me that any child would be such a half-wit as to swallow the stones which we, in our charming fashion, used to spit out forcibly, aiming accurately at our friends...

The more I think of myself in those days, the more horrible I appear.

※　　※　　※

With holly-bark I used to make bird-lime. I never caught a bird on this sticky glue, but I caught myself, and my father and my mother and my little sister.

It was like that old music-hall song, *"When Father Papered the Parlour"* – "You've never seen such a bloomin' family so stuck up before!"

But Gerard, in whose great work I've just looked up the Holly, while admitting that the bird-lime is "marvellous clammy" (and if you eat it – but who would? – "It glueth up the entrails") tells me something I never knew before, that the stickiest bird-lime is made from mistletoe berries, "far exceeding that which is made of holly-bark."

"Some of the Learned," quoth he, "have set down that Misseltoe comes of the dung of a bird called a Thrush, who having fed of the seeds thereof and left his dung upon the tree, whereof was ingendered this berry, a most fit matter to make lime of to intrap and catch birds withall."

※　　※　　※

I trust nobody nowadays wishes to intrap and catch birds withall. There are all too few of them and the thrushes which spread the mistletoe about our apple orchards are scarcer than they have ever been, where I live, anyhow. Another hard winter would hit them badly.

So don't forget to put out all your scraps on your bird-table in the garden. By doing so we may save the lives of up to a million birds a year.

A farmyard relic

The Things they do Say

Any day now the first snowflakes will drift down and we shall say that the old 'oman is plucking her geese ready for Christmas.

Country folk have vivid phrases for every turn of the weather as you'd expect among people who are closely affected by it.

The other night, for instance, we had a "duck's frost," which isn't a frost at all – it means a night of mizzling rain. 'To mizzle' is itself an expressive word.

A very light frost is known as a 'cornerfrost' because it whitens only the sheltered corners of the fields.

We hardly ever speak of thunder, except with reference to the actual storm. Instead we say "there's tempest about."

In hot, sullen weather, when the sky grows dark without any rain, the old men will often say: "It looks like tempest but I reckon it's blight." I think they believe that the sky is really darkened by blight, which, of course, is quite absurd.

❈　❈　❈

The still, heavy weather is favourable to the aphis, and at such times they will sometimes blacken a whole orchard, especially of damsons – for those are their favourite trees.

But the blight doesn't fall out of the sky, or cause the queer darkness-at-noon which occurs now and then during hot summers.

I find that countrymen, despite all that has been written to the contrary, are worse weather-forecasters than intelligent townsmen – and much worse than the Air Ministry's experts.

Indeed, some farmers I know acknowledge this when they privily ring up the nearest Met. Office for one of those free, gratis and astonishingly accurate short-term forecasts.

I have the greatest respect for these Met. scientists, but I do wish they would call their headquarters the weather office instead of the meteorological office.

'Meteorological,' to begin with, is almost impossible to pronounce; it ought to be used as a test for drunkenness!

Secondly, it seems to suggest that it is concerned with the study of meteors, which, of course, it isn't.

And finally, its real, original, Greek derivation ('a discourse about something high in the air') is extremely obscure and is most curiously related to a word *meteorizesthai*, defined as 'to suffer from flatulence,' a very different sort of wind!

※　　※　　※

From the hoity-toity 'meteorology' let us turn to some down-to-earth words, which are suggested to me because we recently killed our household pig.

As you know, in the case of a pig you can eat 'everything but the squeal'; and every piece and fragment of the animal therefore bear the appropriate names – by which the neighbours will not be unwilling to ask for them. "If so be as you 'oodn't be fancying the chitterlings…"

Fordson tractor

Well, we don't fancy the chitterlings, but we very much fancy the 'pig's fry,' which is composed of the liver, lights, heart, etc., and is sometimes called the aslet (or hazelet), sometimes the 'nightcap' and sometimes the 'Tom-hodge.'

The thin membrane or diaphragm, in which one wraps it to make the faggots, is called the apron. The fatty lining of the stomach, from which one renders down the lard, is the leaf; and when all the lard has been melted off it, is know as scratchums or scratchings.

The fat, which comes off the chitterlings is mudgin, or sometimes tippit, the jowl is spoken of as chawl, and the ears and nose, pickled, are 'souse.'

※　　※　　※

Interesting words, but as I said, down-to-earth ones. Yet I wonder whether, had 'chitterlings' not got the association in our minds with innards, it might not equally be a word of endearment – 'You little chitterling!'

We certainly tend to think that particular words have a kind of built-in resemblance to the ideas they stand for, simply because we ourselves are so accustomed to the association.

A good example of this fancy occurs in Aldous Huxley's novel 'Crome Yellow.' His character, old Rowley, points at some swine which are wallowing in mud. 'Look at them sir,' he says. 'Rightly is they called pigs.'

Suffolk lamb

No 'Scholard' but he knew the Answer

Looking through some old papers I came across a curious mathematical problem scribbled on the back of the catalogue of a sale of Live and Dead farming stock.

The date of the sale was late September, 1927; and I in those days was a youth employed as an articled clerk in my uncle's firm of auctioneers.

My job on this particular day was to sit in a little improvised office in a farm shed, receive the sales slips as they were brought in to me by the firm's porter from time to time while the sale went on, make out the individual accounts from them, receive the money and balance up the cash.

All this had to be done at a great pace – I had to work very much as a bookmaker's clerk works – and however fast I went there was always a queue of people who wanted to get away in a hurry, some of them being dealers, pretty rough characters, apt to be bullies when they were impatient, further confusing me with such comments as 'Bloody good clurk you are!'

❋ ❋ ❋

Now the livestock at this particular sale consisted largely of sheep and for that reason the buyers came mainly from the sheep country of Herefordshire, Shropshire and Wales.

In those days quite a few of the hill farmers who had done so well that they could draw a cheque for a thousand pounds or more were nevertheless so illiterate that they were unable to write it out. However I was not aware of that at the time.

When somebody chucked a blank cheque at me on which was only a smudged signature scrawled with a licked indelible pencil and said: 'Go on, fill it in for me: 80 tegs at 84s 6d. – £338' – well, naturally, I said: 'Write out the so-and-so thing yourself.'

Instead of the expected abuse there was dead silence; at last I looked up and in place of the bully I had imagined there was a gentle-looking man with a hurt and extremely embarrassed expression. He whispered quickly; 'Sorry, mister, you see I'm no scholar, and apart from my signature I can't write!'

For the very shame I could not look him in the eyes. I bent low over my desk made out the cheque, and hurriedly passed him the receipt for it.

❋ ❋ ❋

But when the sale was over I went into the beer tent for what I thought was a well-deserved half-pint and there I met the man who couldn't write but who was at least substantial enough to possess £338.

With a shy grin, he said: 'I think you had better have this one with me, mister!'

227

※　　※　　※

He was a sheep farmer from high up in the hills. He hadn't had any education worth speaking of but had made a good deal of money and he certainly had his wits about him as far as sheep dealing was concerned.

It surprised me that a man who couldn't write could do this sum, 80 x 84s 6d.

In a roundabout way so as not to hurt his feelings, I asked him about this, and he confessed to me that he had never learned any 'school' mathematics either.

He could multiply and divide by two and he could add, but that was as far as he could go.

This was the stage where I began to write down the calculation upon the back of the sale catalogue, and this is how it goes:

He puts down 80 in the left-hand column and £4 4s 6d in the right-hand one. He then proceeds to divide the left-hand column by 2 and multiply the right-hand one by 2, thus:-

80	£4 4 6
40	£8 9 0
20	£16 18 0
10	£33 16 0
5	£67 12 0
2	£135 4 0
1	£270 8 0

(In dividing, he takes no notice of odd fractions, as you see. In some extraordinary fashion the sum works out correctly even if he ignores them.)

Next he strikes out all the lines in which the left-hand column contains an even number, so he is left with:-

£67 12 0
£270 8 0
————
£338 0 0
————

All he has to do now is to add up the remaining figures in the right-hand column. They, as you see, amount to £338, which gives him the correct answer to his sum.

❈   ❈   ❈

The thing works. But I am not a very good mathematician and I cannot see why the devil it should work. I am sure there are a lot of real scholars among my readers and I should be fascinated if any of them can send me a proof of this problem, either by algebraic equation or otherwise.

I shall listen for the Mistle-thrush Tonight...

We had a pair of Mistlethrushes which lived in our orchard. The cock sang to us every day from the topmost branch of a very tall pear.

He sang all the louder last March, when his mate was sitting on her nest in the low fork of a sycamore tree. The young were fledged by the time the cuckoo was calling. Then one day I picked up the cock bird dead in our drive.

About a month later I found another dead bird, probably his mate. In neither case was there any sign of injury.

We missed the evening song from the tall perry pear-tree. But yesterday, just before dark I heard it again.

There was a high wind blowing, and at shut of day the black clouds began to roll up from the north-west bringing some flakes of soft snow.

The topmost bough of the pear-tree was tossed by the wind; but there was a mistlethrush clinging to it, and as he clung there he poured his heart out in song.

Not for nothing is the bird called the stormcock.

April brood

He must have been one of the April brood. So nature sees to it that the species goes on.

I shall listen for him tonight and it will please me to think of the young bird with the speckled breast perching and singing in the high top exactly where his father perched and sang.

There's a poem by Thomas Hardy called, I think, 'Proud Songsters.'

These brand-new birds of twelve months growing,
Which a year ago, or less than twain,

No finches were, no nightingales,
Nor thrushes,
But only particles of grain
And earth, and air, and rain.

Dust to dust; and so in an endless cycle.

But I pray this young one may not already be partly composed of some particles of deadly stuff – organochlorines, aldrin and dieldrin, even DDT – which are ingested with poisoned insects, slugs, snails and worms, and which, building up gradually in the tissues, were probably the cause of the deaths of our brand-new songster's father and mother.

❈   ❈   ❈

We have a cat called Sammy Davis Junior which alone among all the cats we have known is both clumsy and rather stupid.

But he is very endearing in spite of, or perhaps because of, these faults.

Sammy, as you can imagine, is not a very good hunter; and up to now his only prey has been young water-rats, creatures even slower on the uptake than he is.

A whole family of these charming rodents grew up in our stream; and they would swim very slowly along under the bank where Sammy would sit for hours, waiting for them.

The bank in places is only six inches above the level of the stream; so it was easy for Sammy to dab with his paw and seize the innocent water-rat before it had time to dive.

We loved the water-rats and disapproved of Sammy's babyish sport.

He did not even eat them, but brought them into the house to show everybody how clever he was before hiding them under a piece of furniture or in a cupboard where they wouldn't be found until they started to smell.

So one day, when my wife saw Sammy coming from the stream with something furry and brown in his jaws, she shouted to me:

"He's got the last of the water-rats! I'll take it away from him."

A moment later I heard her scream.

Sammy's prey this time was not a harmless water-rat, but a fully-grown and very fierce land-rat which thanked her for its release from Sammy's jaws by biting her through the finger.

She let it go and it ran away; Sammy pursued caught and killed it, and got his paw nipped in the process.

Rat-bites are particularly poisonous, and sometimes carry dangerous diseases; so my wife had to go to the hospital to have the wound dressed and disinfected and to be injected with penicillin.

Now she and Sammy both go about with a heroic, wounded-in-battle, ought-to-be-decorated-for-valour kind of an air.

❋　　❋　　❋

Talking of cats and their victims, I heard someone in the pub the other day declaring that one of our local sabbatarians was as bad as 'the man who hung his cats on a Monday.'

How odd that this old saying should have got into our common speech; for I looked it up and it comes from a very obscure source, '*Barnabee's Journal*,' written by Richard Brathwaite about 1650.

> *To Banbury came I, O profane one!*
> *Where I saw a Puritane-one*
> *Hanging of his cat on Monday*
> *For killing of a mouse on Sunday.*

You may carve the Turkey but...

I read somewhere that the Sheriff of Gloucestershire, for some reason, during the reign of Henry III had to supply various contributions towards the King's Christmas festivities.

They included 20 salmon to be made into pies and a number of 'cranes' which may, for all I know, have been herons.

There were no turkeys in England in those days; they didn't arrive until the sixteenth century, and the 'crane' was regarded as an important dish.

Incidentally, in a lordly household, you didn't in the old days 'carve' a heron – or a crane – or a peacock – or a bittern.

According to the *Book of Carving*, printed by Wynkyn de Worde, there were niceties of nomenclature. You were said to 'dismember' a heron, to 'display' a crane, to 'disfigure' a peacock to 'unjoint' a bittern and so on.

It was correct to 'wing' a partridge or a quail but if the bird was a pigeon or a woodcock you were said to 'thye' it.

You would 'break' a deer, 'sauce' a capon, 'frush' a chicken, 'unbrace' a mallard, 'unlace' a coney, 'mine' a plover, 'splat' a pike 'chine' a salmon, 'string' a lamprey, 'splay' a bream, 'side' a haddock, 'tush' a barbel, 'culpon' a trout, 'fine' a chub, 'trassen' an eel, 'barb' a lobster.

And you could 'undertraunch' a porpoise – if you were unfortunate enough to have to eat a porpoise, which must have made rather a formidable contribution towards the Christmas cheer.

※　※　※

I daresay any kind of meat was welcome in those times before the rotation of crops and the provision of winter feed for stock.

During the early part of the winter all except the precious breeding stock had to be killed off, so that Christmas was certainly the last great feast.

233

After that there would be nothing in the way of fresh meat until the spring, unless you were a country gentleman who was lucky enough to have a dovecote, or a monk fortunate in his stew pond, or a landlord with a chance of laying hands on some sort of wild game.

For most people most of the time the only meat ever tasted during the dark and bitter months of the year was heavily salted and pickled and probably pretty high into the bargain.

Wine or strong beer was not a luxury, it was practically a necessity; you wouldn't have been able to eat much of the salted and peppered meat without it.

❋　　❋　　❋

Aware, no doubt, of the short commons to come, people made the most enormous feasts during the last few weeks of the year.

If you should read the diaries of Parson Woodforde, a country rector who held livings in Somerset and Norfolk during the latter years of the eighteenth century, you will be simply staggered by the quantity of food which he managed to eat and the assortment of wines and ales and whatnot which he was able to consume.

❋　　❋　　❋

And here's a menu (from the Sussex Archaeological Society's Transactions) for Christmas dinner served in 1707 to the thirteen guests of Squire Timothy Burrell of Cuckfield:

> Plumm Pottage
> Calve's Head and Bacon
> Goose
> Pig
> Roast beef, sirloin
> Veale, sirloin
> Boil'd beef, a clod
> Two Bak'd Puddings
> Three dishes of Minced Pyes

Two Capons
Two dishes of Tarts
Two pullets.

❖　　❖　　❖

You will notice that even the Squire didn't have turkey. He could have done, presumably, but according to the old rhyme:

Turkeys, Carpes, Hops, Piccerels and Beere
Came into England all in one yeere

– the year being round about 1520, so these delectable things arrived more or less at the same time as the less agreeable Reformation.

I don't' know whether there is any truth in the rhyme. I have always believed that the pike (or pickerel) was a native fish; the carp probably *did* come over from the Continent about the same time as we got hops from Holland and gave up flavouring our ale with Ground Ivy.

As for the turkey, it doesn't come from Turkey, of course, but from North and Central America. I believe the first of these birds were brought over by the Spaniards from Mexico about 1519, but it was probably a couple of hundred years or so before they began to be associated with Christmas dinners.

A-gooding they would go

Round about Christmas-time, we are told, the poorer women had a custom of 'going a-gooding' – when they collected holly and ivy and went round the houses offering these as presents, for the Christmas decorations.

They expected, and generally received, more valuable Christmas boxes in return.

Now, by chance, the other day I came across a mention of this custom in an old book, published in 1794. Pointing out that the previous winter had been exceptionally mild, it observed:

The women who went a-gooding might in return for alms, have presented their benefactors with palms and bunches of primroses.

Pussy-willows and primroses in bloom in late December! That must have been the mildest winter since Englishmen began to keep count of the seasons.

❈   ❈   ❈

Modern historians are at great pains to point out to us that most of the traditional trappings of 'the old English Christmas' are really Germanic and were introduced by Prince Albert.

But this is sheer nonsense. If you read about Christmas-tides in the writings of the 17th century and earlier, you will learn that folk decorated their houses, sung carols, ate Christmas Puddings and mince pies, let off primitive crackers, bought in Yule logs, and kissed under the mistletoe, much as we do nowadays.

Prince Albert may, for all I know, have introduced the Christmas tree; I've never come across a mention of it in the Elizabethan or Restoration plays.

❈   ❈   ❈

Churches were decorated as well as houses, in the old days, though in most parts the mistletoe was forbidden to enter there,

236

being considered a 'heathenish and profane plant,' possibly because of its supposed association with the Druids and their sacrifices.

The ivy, according to a very old carol, seems to have been used to decorate the *outside* of houses, and the holly was brought *inside*.

This carol charmingly described the ivy as the owl's special tree, probably because owls often use its evergreen cover for their daytime perch. I have modernised some of the words:

> *Ivy hath berries as black as any sloe,*
> *There come the owl and eat them as they go…*
> *Holly hath birdes, a full fair flock,*
> *The nightingale, the popinjay, the gentle Laverock.*
> *But good Ivy! What birdes hast thou?*
> *None but the howlet that cries 'How! How!'*

❈　　❈　　❈

Mincepies are mentioned in Ben Jonson's *Masque of Christmas* (1616); and Christmas puddings must have come in not much later, for the Puritans inveighed against them, as they did against all jolly things.

At one time the clergy were forbidden to taste the pudding; and one of the Puritan writers went so far as to describe it as 'an invention of the scarlet woman of Babylon, and a hodge-podge of superstition, popery, the devil and all his words.'

Perhaps he wrote that on Boxing day, when he was suffering from the effects of having eaten too much!